# CONTENTS

## AUTHORS' BIOGRAPHIES

**NICK LEESON** became known the world over as the 'rogue trader' when he famously brought down Barings Bank in 1995. Sentenced to six and a half years in prison, he served the majority of his jail term in Singapore's notoriously harsh Tanah Merah complex. In 1998 he was diagnosed with colon cancer, but has since recovered to take a degree in psychology. He remarried in 2004 and now lives with his wife Leona, his stepchildren Kersty and Alex and his son Mackensey on the West Coast of Ireland.

**IVAN TYRRELL** is the principal of MindFields College and has been a director of the European Therapy Studies Institute since 1993. He also works as a human givens therapist – treating mainly depression and anxiety disorders – and coaches senior executives on applying these principles in large organisations. He co-authored with Joe Griffin the book *Human Givens: A New Approach to Emotional Health and Clear Thinking* – which has been described by *New Scientist* as 'a quiet revolution'. Ivan lives with his family in the Sussex countryside.

## ACKNOWLEDGEMENTS AND DEDICATION

The day I left England in April 1992 to work for Barings in Singapore started an emotional journey that has now thankfully come to an end. Without the support and help of certain people I don't think I would have been able to complete that journey. No one has been more influential than my lawyer, now my friend, Stephen Pollard, who pushed, cajoled and often dragged me through some of the most difficult events in my life. I am forever grateful for the help and support he offered me and my family. My family and friends were equally fantastic throughout the whole episode and, although too numerous to mention here, I owe them all a debt of gratitude.

I'd like to thank my editor, Kerri Sharp, who has been fantastic throughout the editing process, along with the Executive Chairman of Virgin Books, Adrian Sington, and my agent Keith Bishop for their belief in the book and in initiating this project. Ivan Tyrrell was a fascinating person to meet at this stage of my life and the conversations we had have given me a greater understanding of why certain things happened and why I reacted in the manner I did. That knowledge leaves me far better equipped to face the future.

Completing this book leaves me refreshed and eager to embrace what lies ahead. I now have a new family that loves me for who I am, a new baby, and hopefully endless opportunities.

For Leona, Kersty, Alex and Mackensey

# Preface by Ivan Tyrrell

Nick Leeson's true-life story is quite exceptional – a modern day *Arabian Nights* adventure. From being an unremarkable working-class lad from Watford, in a few short years he gained access to enormous riches, worked hard, played hard, fell in love, became corrupted by circumstances, cunningly lived a lie in order to maintain his position, brought down an ancient financial empire, achieved worldwide notoriety as a consequence, went on the run, was caught and imprisoned for several years in a far-off land, felt abandoned by his wife, suffered cruelty and solitary confinement in a concrete box, became a shadow of his former self, escaped death by cancer, returned to the world and rebuilt his life a changed man.

His career is a potent reminder of the remarkable swings of fortune any one of us can experience during our life. On the one hand, it is an emblem for human weakness and folly and, on the other, an example of how it is possible to endure extremes of misfortune and survive. For ten years, stress continually affected his physical and mental health, yet he found ways to get through it and is now healthy and flourishing, though marked for life by what he did.

A few months after leaving prison, to bring structure back into his life, Nick began a psychology degree course. In doing that he became interested in how continual high stress levels can affect physical and mental health and he wanted to write a book that not only told his complete personal story but would also explore what stress in the modern world actually means. He also wanted to offer insights and tips to help other people who feel overwhelmed by life's difficulties.

The executive chairman of Virgin Books, Adrian Sington, thought such a book would be valuable for all sorts of reasons and suggested I help Nick write it. Adrian introduced us in London. Soon afterwards we found ourselves beginning work on this book in Galway, on the West Coast of Ireland, where Nick now lives. By then he had thoroughly read a book I co-authored with Joe Griffin: *Human Givens: A New Approach to Emotional Health and Clear Thinking*. The book gave him a higher level of understanding about why his life had developed the way it had.

To understand more about Nick Leeson's remarkable life, we talked about the impossible stress he has experienced, and how he brought himself back from the brink of despair and a life-threatening illness. These conversations begin in Chapter 3, where we examine how our need for status can get out of hand and what happens when we are desperate to live up to our own – or others' – expectations of us. Our aim was to reveal the interplay between the givens of human nature and how stressed Nick became when his life started to go wrong. What we unravelled is relevant to everyone, particularly those who feel stressed or adrift in the modern world.

# chapter 1
# My Story So Far

How can anyone call me lucky?

Imagine having spent four and a half years in one of the world's toughest prisons after being responsible for the biggest financial scandal of the century, going through a divorce while behind bars and then, to cap it all, being diagnosed with cancer. They used to call me lucky when I was on the trading floor of the Singapore Monetary Exchange; I'm not sure what their definition of unlucky was but it must have been pushing at the extremities of misfortune. The rumours of my infallibility on the trading floor were once the stuff of legend in financial circles. By the time I was incarcerated, they had probably been replaced by a moral fable that regaled how my demise had been so complete and so final.

Luckily, fate determined there was more in store for me. I survived the adversities of incarceration, life-threatening illness and isolation to tell this story – a story of extreme stress brought about by naked ambition and recklessness, and of the recovery and change for good that it is possible to effect, even after going through dire circumstances.

Since *Rogue Trader* was published in 1996, I often felt that I wanted to write another book chronicling the drastic events that transpired once I was extradited to Singapore. As I write this, it is ten years since the collapse of Barings Bank –

a good time to look back at those events with a more mature outlook and a greater understanding of why things happened the way they did. For me, writing has been cathartic. Every day during my jail term in Singapore I kept a diary, and in many ways it became my bible. I'd read it often, sometimes a few times a day. I'd refer back to it and reappraise the situation; one doesn't always get it right the first time one's words tumble out on to paper. And I never fabricated any element of my experience. I wanted a full and honest account of all the emotions I was feeling and how they affected me.

Being locked up for 23 hours a day for a good part of my sentence gave me a lot of time to think. Churning over a negative period in your life can be self-defeating, adding to your worries rather than giving solutions – however, you can turn this to your advantage by getting those thoughts down on paper and confronting them. It was doing this that kept me sane and gave me hope but, most of all, it supported me through the entire period I was in jail. In fact, confronting your fears and worries through writing may be the most accessible and cheapest form of therapy available. It worked for me, as I closed doors on episodes of my former life and opened them on to new ones.

It was galling, then, that the prison authorities made me shred all my journals on the day I left Singapore. It was one of the most upsetting things I have ever had to do, feeding page after page of my innermost thoughts into the jaws of the machine until none remained. I knew there would be a new life and better times ahead of me, but I felt I would somehow be less equipped without my memories. However, the basic content of those journals would see a new incarnation – in this book.

It was the chance to be involved in writing about stress that enabled me to access those initial thoughts and experiences. The shredded journals were an invaluable tool for me during my incarceration but I had read them so many times that it was not difficult to recount their contents. With the opportunity of writing a book that dealt with stress, I could focus my thoughts and memories into something more specific. After leaving prison I took a degree in psychology. It was the part of the syllabus that covered stress that interested me the most, due to my own experiences of being under immense pressure and the ill health I suffered while in jail. However, the academic nature of the course meant that the subject was dealt with in terms of its clinical cause and effect and, for me, didn't capture the personal experience or intensity of emotion one feels while suffering intense pressure. Neither did it look at the sociological factors that contribute to stress.

There can be little dispute that stress has a significant negative impact on the well-being of both the individual and the organisation they work for. Ever-growing research initiatives have made the link time and again between stress and incidences of heart disease, alcoholism, mental breakdown, job dissatisfaction, accidents, family problems and particular forms of cancer. Certain countries, the US and Finland, for example, are showing a decline in some stress-related illnesses such as heart disease and alcoholism. The UK is not even coming close to matching their achievements with a figure of 66,000 people reporting work-related heart disease in 2003/4. The World Health Organisation recently published figures indicating that not only is the UK near the top of the world league table in terms of fatality due to heart disease, but it is also extending that lead with ongoing yearly increases in the statistics. A survey carried out by the Health and Safety Executive found that in the period 2003/4 over half a million Britons believed they were experiencing work-related stress to a level that was making them ill. The Stress and Health at Work Study (SHAW) reports that nearly one in five of all workers thought their job was very or extremely stressful. The indirect costs to employers of stress-related illnesses are staggering but it is a difficult thing to quantify. Employers rarely attempt to estimate such costs and employees take leave for a variety of complaints that do not mention the word 'stress' on their sick notes – even though stress may be the root cause of an impaired immune system or, for example, a migraine or back pain. Instead, absenteeism, high labour turnover and low productivity are seen as an inevitable part of running a business and little is done to target the problem at its root cause.

Although no two individuals' circumstances are ever exactly alike, I believe many of today's sufferers of extreme stress have fallen victim in some way to *unrealistic expectations*. This is certainly true in my case, as the first conversational section in Chapter 3 will demonstrate. Of course, it would be foolish to declare that stress is a new condition; our ancestors worked punishing hours and lived in conditions that would be considered intolerable by modern western standards. If we consider the hardship that was brought about by war and extreme poverty as recently as sixty years ago, the average daily life of most people in the UK in 2000s is one of luxury. But with the conveniences of the technological age has come the inconvenience of having to be a success in an increasingly competitive market or, rather, the threat of the ignominious state of being seen as a failure. Many people are growing up conditioned to think they can 'have it all' – that they will have the perfect lives as sold to them by relentless lifestyle advertising and will not have to delay gratification in accessing the material goods they want. We have also become neurotic about checking our status – to see how we measure on the rung of achievement. Any perceived notion of failure is bound to cause distress when we are striving to maintain a face of accomplishment and acquisition to our peers and our families. We are expected to do well, to keep climbing up the social ladder, while the truth is that a more simple life can often provide greater contentment.

In 1992, at the age of 25, I was on that ladder. I had the world at my feet. My mother died suddenly when I was 20, and that was a huge blow, but I was extremely successful at work, being paid a lot of money for doing a job I loved, and had recently got married; the prospects really couldn't have been much better. But in less than three years everything went haywire and I somehow managed to force the majority of life's more stressful events into a very short period of time. Problems in the workplace, stresses associated with relocating to a new country, financial and marriage difficulties littered that period, and laid the foundations of a life-threatening illness that was to erupt a few years later. The ripple effect of my trying to cover up a few minor accounting errors spiralled into the collapse of the world's oldest private bank and saw me serving time in jail while seriously ill. It was chaos theory played out to an extreme consequence.

Most working people would say stress is a major feature in their lives. Although its causes and manifestations may be particular to each individual's circumstances, I do think there is continuity in the coping mechanisms that can be used to help overcome its effects. Although my experiences – and the situations I got myself into – have been more extreme than most people will face, I hope the fact that I managed to pull through it all and survive will provide hope to anyone who is unduly stressed with a life event of their own. If nothing else, I must be the living embodiment of the declaration that what doesn't kill you can only make you stronger.

I didn't want this book to be laden with scientific jargon; I wanted a book that was pragmatic and practical – something a wide audience could read to gain an insight into the chronically debilitating effects of extreme stress brought about by the need for status (and other factors, such as an inability to limit risk-taking behaviour) and offer effective ways of coping with it. In this book you will not find a dry list of all the medical theories of stress, or some miracle plan that will restore your life to a trouble-free zone of calm. This is primarily an account of what stress did to me on a personal and physical level, and how I used the innate resources available to us all to help me recover from its worst affects.

The book is written in collaboration with experiential psychologist Ivan Tyrrell, whose approach to the subject is based on the 'human givens' model of life. On reading the book he co-authored with Joe Griffin, I was struck by the simplicity of his approach and the ease with which I could absorb the theories. The idea that we all have innate needs and it is when these needs are not met that stress manifests itself made a lot of sense to me. I confess to being somewhat dogmatic and stoical in my opinions and I rarely change them, but as we spoke about my life I found that I was reforming my opinions of why I had behaved the way I did.

The conversation was illuminating and significantly changed the way I looked at that difficult period of my life. Ivan and Joe Griffin's book mentions in the first few pages that 'there is always more to learn and understand. It is this stretching process – as our brains continually resculpt through new learning – that makes us such an adaptable species.'

I'm certainly still learning but I would like to think my experiences have taught me how to tackle life's problems in a more efficient manner. I have never felt more confident than I do today that I am able to cope with whatever may confront me in the future. I have not always had this confidence; prior to all of the adversity I would have run away from a problem rather than deal with it, being a bit of a coward. Any confidence I portrayed was an act, masking how nervous or scared I really was, but I now truly believe I am able to deal with just about anything.

Stress can be tackled either by reducing the pressure, by increasing our coping strategies, or by a combination of the two. But putting the stressor into perspective is an important first step. We all have these innate inner resources to deal with the most extreme and adverse of conditions, even if most of us are unaware of them until they are needed. The snag, unfortunately, is that these coping mechanisms are not always readily accessible. We are not taught them; we have to find or experience them, and usually through adversity. But with a bit of nurture and education these resources will become useful allies by which we can counteract other stressful events that may come along.

I lucked out on the coping strategies. I would have known nothing about them before using them but when they were called upon, in my darkest moments, they were already there. I think that learning about coping mechanisms may go a long way to explain why I am so laidback and relaxed about things these days. I really do feel as though I have found an inner strength to cope with pretty much anything life can throw at me. I am more inclined to think that it's not the things that stress us that cause problems; it's the way in which we react to them. It is important to remember that when your temper rises or you feel emotional you have within you the power to react in a way that is not detrimental to your well-being. Spending day after day undergoing the demeaning process of being stripped naked in jail for a full body search taught me that there are some things one just has to accept. The first few times it happened I'd be full of rage but I soon had to face the facts.

However frustrating it may be at the time, there are some things in life you have the ability to affect, and there are others you do not. You cannot allow the things you have no control over to worry you unduly. Prison teaches you that quicker than any counselling course, but it's not so difficult a lesson that we can't all see it with just a couple of minutes' reflection. The warder didn't really want to humiliate me; he knew I wasn't going to smuggle anything out of the workshop, but a strip search was one of the rules. Everything in my life is now separated into simple formulae – into the things I can influence and things I can't. Anything in the former can exert stress on me, anything in the latter cannot. This significantly reduces the number of potential stressors in my life but, as you journey through the book, you'll see that I further subdivide everything into 'absolutes' and 'imponderables'.

Having cancer is an absolute. I'm aware of the ramifications but it doesn't stress me unduly. I can cope with it; I look after my health and I take all the necessary precautions. On the other hand, being aware of the possible genetic predisposition to cancer, I worry that I may have passed this hereditary probability on to my son, Mackensey. Thinking about that is intolerable and is an example of an 'imponderable' – something that I do worry about, even though that worry may be futile, but I can turn that worry to both of our advantages by being aware of the signs and symptoms of the disease. Again, with effective coping strategies in place, one can overcome the greatest trials. Information is an important tool in anyone's repertoire. Although the natural tendency is for people to avoid thinking about the 'the worst', in not facing the facts of a problem, I am convinced that a 'head in the sand' reaction puts people at a disadvantage.

Hopefully, if you are suffering from stress, this book will help point to some of its root causes and also offer analyses and coping strategies for minimising its worst effects. Each chapter begins with an introduction from me that outlines my experience of that chapter's main subject. This is followed by the conversational sections where both Ivan Tyrrell and I tease out the heart of the issue, putting the causes into some sociological context before offering practical advice and tips on coping with that particular stressor.

The book has been a fantastic journey for me, revisiting painful episodes in my life but applying a new approach to their understanding. We all feel we know what stress is but the personal experience of it can be debilitating and injurious to our health, our loved ones and our zest for life. The solution lies is finding those coping mechanisms. Hopefully this book will help.

# chapter 2
## WHAT IS STRESS? —
# needs, resources and human givens

The week we began work on this book, Nick's wife Leona gave birth to their first child together, a nine-pound boy called Mackensey. This coincidence allows me to illustrate what we psychologists mean by the term 'human givens'. Like all of us, Mackensey came into the world with an enormous amount of innate knowledge that has evolved over millions of years. For example, he knew straight away how to suckle at his mother's breast. He knew how to build rapport with whoever was holding him. He knew how to draw attention to himself whenever he felt hungry or uncomfortable. All this knowledge, and much more, was programmed into him from Nick's and Leona's genes. We recognise that this knowledge is there through the two ways it is expressed: as physical and emotional *needs*, and as innate human *abilities* (or *resources*).

Innate *physical* needs are obvious: air to breathe, food and drink for nutrition, sufficient warmth for comfort, and the space to move about and grow. When the need for nutrition, for example, is matched up to a mother's milk, all is well. But, when such innate needs are not met, we are in trouble. We can all see what happens when children are starved, or fed on a diet of harmful foods, or are not allowed to play in ways that encourage physical activity. We can see immediately when a child is underweight, overweight, hyperactive or listless – whether it has a healthy glow or a sickly pallor. The damage is obvious.

When the inner, *emotional* needs of a child are not met, the damage is just as severe but not always as easy to pin down. Every emotional need nature has given us is a partial pattern within us seeking completion in the outside world. It can only be completed when it is matched up to appropriate stimuli in the environment. For example, if we feel lonely and have a need for a friend, that incomplete pattern in us drives us to make a friend. When we make a friend, the feeling of aloneness goes away because the innate pattern that was expressed as a need is now completed in the environment. Because our *emotional* needs are partial patterns, and we are driven to try and match them up to complete them in the outside world, every child and adult automatically tries to do this.

So what exactly are these emotional needs? Well, they are all connected to survival and our continuing evolution. That is to say, they are related to sex and procreation, our relationships to wider groups (we are an intensely social species) and our sense of meaning and purpose. These inner patterns force us to seek safety and security, get attention from others, make emotional connections to others, have an intimate close relationship to at least one other person, have volition (to feel one has some control over events), obtain a degree of status within one's family and peer groups, have competence in some areas (which ensures that low self-esteem doesn't develop), and be 'stretched' by how we live and what we do (because being physically and/or mentally stretched gives meaning and purpose to our lives – a busy brain is a healthy brain). All these emotional needs have to be met in a balanced way if a child or adult is to develop well and fulfil his or her potential.

We know these innate needs – the human givens – are important because research shows that, if any one of them is not matched up by what happens to a person in the environment they find themselves in, they become emotionally disturbed. If this is not corrected, this eventually takes a major toll on that individual's physical and mental health.

'Stress' is what happens when these needs are not being met in our life. Only then do we become anxious, angry or depressed. And it's when we try to compensate for what's missing that other neurotic symptoms such as attention-seeking or addictive behaviour arise.

We can all recognise this when we think about it. Every baby needs warmth, quiet times to sleep, proper food, comfort and good-quality attention to feel safe. It soon shows signs of stress if these needs are not met. This is why every baby is programmed to connect with its mother from the moment it is born. It 'knows' it is totally dependent on her and must do this to survive. Without good parenting it will not flourish and can even die.

Every adult has innate needs that have to be met too. People become distressed if they are lonely, insecure, feel out of control of some important aspects of their life (for example, their finances, relationships or health), have status taken away from them or are not stretched to learn in the way they

live their lives. Fortunately, to help us meet our needs, nature
has given us a wealth of resources, such as:

- ▸ the ability to learn (and thus add new knowledge
  to that which we were given to start the process off)
- ▸ the ability to remember
- ▸ the ability to build a rapport, empathise and connect
  with others
- ▸ a powerful imagination
- ▸ the ability to acquire language and communicate
- ▸ the ability to think things out, analyse and plan
- ▸ the ability to understand the world unconsciously –
  through pattern-matching and metaphor. The brain
  even has the capacity to calm down and become aware
  that it is aware and, when we attain that state, be more
  objective and connected to the greater reality.

Another important human given is that every night we dream
(even if we don't remember doing so). Dreaming is nature's
way of discharging stress. We don't have to remember our
dreams for them to do their work. While we sleep they dis-
charge the emotions aroused by expectations in the daytime
that were not acted out in the real world, and thus 'de-aroused'.
Without the outlet provided by dreaming, these emotions
would remain charged up in the autonomic nervous system.

So, inner resources, like physical and emotional needs, are
also 'human givens'. They are the tools for survival that
nature bequeaths to each new baby – a form of knowledge.
All subsequently acquired skills and knowledge are what we
gain through consciously experiencing the world – what
people usually call learning and remembering.

Little Mackensey Leeson's life story, like that of everyone on the planet, will be made up of the sum of the way he matches up his innate needs in the environment, and how he uses the resources nature has given him to add new knowledge to what he already 'knows'. How this happens will determine how well his life develops.

## WHAT HAPPENS TO US WHEN WE ARE STRESSED?

Whenever we are prevented from getting our innate physical or emotional needs met the brain reacts as if it is under threat and triggers various adaptive survival responses – it activates something called the *autonomic nervous system.* Without our being consciously aware of it most of the time, this system controls organs, muscles and processes within the body such as blood pressure, heartbeat and digestion. In emergencies, and when we feel under stress, it switches on the body's automatic 'fight or flight' programme by regulating the output of two stress hormones: cortisol and adrenalin. These are the chemicals that help us to cope with change. Adrenalin alerts us and maintains our readiness for action by increasing our heart rate and blood pressure and mobilising our energy reserves. It also makes extra energy available by switching off systems that we don't need, such as digestion and the higher brain centres. Cortisol, by contrast, works more slowly, replenishing energy supplies and alerting the immune system to possible bacterial or viral injury. When there are no emergencies the autonomic nervous system allows us to 'rest and digest'.

In the short run, this system serves us well. But if the stress hormones triggered by the real or imagined threats (stressors) are not used promptly, for example by running away from danger, some or all of the following symptoms will appear:

## STRESS WARNING SIGNALS

### Physical symptoms

► pounding heart
► headaches
► sweaty palms
► indigestion
► skin rashes
► shortness of breath
► holding of breath
► cold hands
► sleeplessness
► too much sleep
► fatigue
► nausea
► diarrhoea
► stomach tightness
► muscle tightness
► pain

### Emotional symptoms

► mood swings
► irritability
► depressed mood
► anxiety
► lack of sense of humour

- abrasiveness
- hostile attitude
- nervousness
- irrationalily
- loss of direction
- cynicism

**Mental symptoms**
- forgetfulness
- loss of concentration
- poor judgement
- disorganisation
- fuzzy perception
- confusion
- lack of interest in pleasurable activities
- deterioration in ability to calculate (maths)
- difficulty in thinking
- diminished fantasy life
- negative self-talk

These symptoms result from the way that the mind and body respond to the surge of bio-chemicals released by the autonomic nervous system when it feels under threat. If a stressful situation doesn't continue for too long, the body internally rebalances itself, a process called homeostasis, and little harm is done. But if someone is overwhelmed by disturbing events they feel they have no control over and experience stress symptoms for a long period (chronic), they will suffer impaired physical and mental health. Their stress hormones begin to eat away at the immune system, opening the way to infection, cancer and major disease – their body slowly begins to kill itself.

## ARE STRESS PROBLEMS INCREASING?

Human beings have always been subject to stressors. Human history is largely one of struggle against terrible odds; disease, famine, war and endless work from dawn to dusk to survive drove the majority of our ancestors to early graves. So people have never been stress-free. The difference today is that our brains have more information to process than ever before. There is a greater variety of stressors we have to deal with simply because we are more aware of what is going on in the world; the pace of change is increasing so rapidly in the modern environment that it is harder to get some of our basic emotional needs met in balanced ways. There is a direct link between the dramatic rise in the rates of most forms of mental illness and the growth in the numbers of stressed people in the population.

Even a newborn baby can suffer if its emotional needs are not met properly. Raised stress levels, caused by emotional neglect – for example, if it's part of a dysfunctional family, perhaps subjected to almost continuous loud noise, such as a blaring TV – inhibits normal development. One in five children in the UK is said to be starting their school day in an emotionally disturbed state and many schools now have a 'calm down' period to allow children with aggressive home environments to adjust to the classroom atmosphere. Emotional disturbance in young people comes about because they were not nurtured, cuddled and quietly comforted for long periods as babies, an activity that produces a higher set point of serotonin (the chemical colloquially called the emotional brake). Children who miss out on this nurture grow up with less tolerance for stressful life events, an inability to delay gratification and a hunger to get their innate emotional needs met over and above the needs of others – which is manifested to the outside world as greater selfishness.

It is because we are individually conditioned by our upbringing and life experiences, and therefore have different expectations, that some people break down more easily in the face of demands while others appear to thrive when confronted with similar challenges. But, sooner or later, the mechanisms for adaptation in every brain can be overwhelmed by too much change and challenge, particularly in the face of continued violence, as in wartime.

One in five people rates their work as very stressful and many relationships founder due to stress in the home. Clearly, the modern human brain, which took millions of years to evolve, is having difficulty adjusting to a world unimaginable just fifty years ago. Our speeded-up lives are putting enormous pressures on both children and adults. And, although the majority cope well, the number of breakdowns caused by stress – in relationships, families, organisations and at work – is rising fast.

The flight-or-fight response, which evolved in the distant past to mobilise us to deal directly with physical threats, is in modern times almost always activated by threats conjured up by our imaginations and lifestyles. This is because the brain's limbic system, which mobilises our stress hormones to help us survive, cannot distinguish between real threats and imagined ones. So when we 'catastrophise' our difficulties with money, health problems, an overcritical partner, underemployment, or ruminate about unfair pressure at work, or fume in traffic jams, our mind and body is suffused with chemicals like adrenalin which bring about rapid heart rate, increased respiration, dry mouth, moist palms and tense muscles, even though we are not having to run away or fight. Such responses, which were appropriate when we were prey to wild animals or an enemy tribe, don't help us much in the modern world. They hurtle around our systems while we sit stationary at desks, on trains and in front of the television, causing us to obsess about our condition. The imagination is a powerful problem-solving tool but, when we misuse it to fantasise disaster, it can hurl us to our wits' end.

Yet we are not entirely at the mercy of ancient automatic survival instincts. We can use our imagination in positive ways to change the way we react and improve the way we adapt to unprecedented challenges that cause us to feel stress. After all, adapting to changing circumstances is essential for survival and mental health. Our ancestors could attest to that!

A popular view of stress is that we are passive, helpless victims of it. Stressors of all sorts, from a death in the family, losing our job, divorce or imprisonment to mislaying our car keys or commuting on an unreliable train service, attack us, and can result in depression and even disease. A stressor, according to this view, is like a germ that causes infection. The answer is generally thought to be: avoid stressors as much as possible and take it easy. But this is the wrong approach and one that is not practical if we need to survive the rigours of daily life. Stress does *not* result simply from exposure to events in the environment. It is how we react to adversity, our *expectations* of life, coupled with whatever mental and physical resources we have available to cope with challenges, which influence the outcome much more than the raw event itself. We actually need stressors in order to stretch ourselves and grow.

Nick's introduction tells how he experienced a number of life's most stressful events in a short period of time: the death of his mother, relocating his job across the world to an alien environment, lawbreaking, living a lie, being found out, loss of status, imprisonment, divorce, major illness. He coped with each stressor as best he could in the moment but, as a young man in his early twenties, immersed in the heady world of financial wheeling and dealing where risk-taking is part of the work, he took a risk too many, thus diverting his life's journey down a path which made him infamous and brought him much physical and mental suffering (to say nothing of the suffering of people who lost large amounts of money as a result of his actions). Throughout he was determined to prove his worth. But the harder he struggled to make things right, the worse the mess became, although for three years only he knew this. The major stress of living a lie, and (as most men in such a situation would find) being unable to admit his mistakes and offload or discuss his worries with colleagues, employers or even his wife, led to his artificial world famously crashing down around him.

Several people in the financial world have said to me, when discussing what happened to Nick Leeson, words to the effect of 'There, but for the grace of God, go I.' It's easy with hindsight to cite negative characteristics such as recklessness or stupidity to 'explain' the fall from grace of Nick Leeson. But what happened to this hard-working, personable young man of above-average intelligence, who wanted to enjoy the status success in his chosen career would bring, could have happened to almost anyone. Stress raises our emotions and emotional arousal can make us stupid.

It is equally easy to plough on dealing with our own, perhaps more mundane, stress-inducing problems, and forget to stand back and take stock so as to be prepared for the stressors that will inevitably come our way and deal with them without being overwhelmed. It cannot be said too often that *it is in the way we deal with life's inevitable stressors that determines whether we stay afloat or become swamped by problems.* Most of us will not be in the position to wreck a major financial institution, but the repercussions of avoiding responsibility can be catastrophic in relative degrees. Things can get out of hand very quickly in any business or relationship situation, once the first weaknesses appear. It is useful to take stock of the common stress-inducing life events from time to time. To help you do this, we have included the Life Stress Test. Fill in the chart on the following pages to assess the intensity of the challenges you face.

## LIFE STRESS TEST

Each event in the following list of stressful events in your life over the last two years is given a different rating by psychologists to show, on average, the pressure that each one adds to your current mental and physical health. Sit back and take a moment to review your life over the past two years. Then work through the list and tally up those events that have happened to you, or are taking place in your life now. If the same thing happened more than once, add the number again (e.g. if you had three holidays that would be thirteen times three). When you have finished, total up the score.

- Death of a spouse 100
- Divorce 73
- Marital (or any other major intimate relationship) separation 65
- Detention in prison or other institution 63
- Death of a close family member (including a child) 63
- Suffering severe bullying 60
- Major personal injury or illness 53
- Getting married 50
- Moving home (house buying) 50
- Being fired from work or made redundant 50
- Caring for an elderly or sick relative 47
- Marital reconciliation 45
- Major change in health or behaviour of a family member 44
- Pregnancy 40
- Sexual difficulty 40
- Gaining a new family member through adoption or remarriage 39
- Major business changes 39
- Major change in financial state 38
- Death of a close friend 37
- Change of occupation 36
- Increase in marital discord (arguments etc.) 35
- Taking on a mortgage 35

- ► Foreclosure on a mortgage or loan  30
- ► Major increase or decrease in responsibility at work  29
- ► Son or daughter leaving home  29
- ► Trouble with in-laws  29
- ► Daily, time-consuming stressful commuting  28
- ► Spouse begins or stops work  26
- ► Start or leave school/college  26
- ► Change in living conditions (building work on home etc.)  25
- ► Major change of personal habits  24
- ► Troubles with superior or boss at work  23
- ► Major change in working hours or conditions  20
- ► Major change in usual type and/or amount of recreation  19
- ► Major change in social activities  18
- ► Major purchase (car, boat or other big item)  17
- ► Major change in quality of sleep  16
- ► Major change in number of family get-togethers  15
- ► Major change in eating habits  15
- ► Holiday away  13
- ► Observing Christmas or other seasonal holiday  12
- ► Minor violations of the law (speeding ticket etc.)  11

**Total the value for those you have ticked
to find your overall stress score.**

*This scale gives a rough guide to the life pressures you are facing.
Depending on your coping skills, or lack of them, this scale can predict
the likelihood that you will fall victim to stress-related emotional
disturbance – anxiety disorders, depression, anger etc. – and/or physical
illnesses ranging from tension headaches, migraines, acid indigestion,
ulceration, polymyalgia and skin problems to serious illnesses like cancer.*

## Life Stress Scores
- ► **0–149** Low susceptibility to stress-related illness.
- ► **150–299** Medium susceptibility to stress-related illness.
  You need to take action to lower your stress levels.
- ► **300 and over** High susceptibility to stress-related illness.
  Do something about your life NOW before a serious illness
  erupts or an affliction becomes worse.

## STRESS AND THE EMOTIONS

If you were to ask the next ten people you met 'How do you deal with stress?' you would be likely to get ten different answers. Although there are patterns in how we respond, each of us approaches life's challenges with a set of responses shaped by our genetic heritage, our life experiences and our perceptions of how we view the actual situation we are dealing with. Frequently, when caught up in a demanding situation, we are not consciously aware of our emotional response to it. We may ignore it by choice, because it might interfere with our rationale for doing something. At work, for example, when faced with a request by our employer to do something which goes against our basic value system, our intuitive reaction may go something like: 'I don't want to do this, but I need the money so I'll just keep my head down and get on with it.' The cost of examining our feelings about it would threaten our equilibrium by creating internal conflict. Or we may be unaware of our emotional response to a situation because we have just never taken the time to think about it.

It is vitally important to our sense of control and therefore our emotional balance that we are aware of the impact of different stresses and strains that life can present. An awareness of how we intuitively respond is the first step in self-awareness.

## STRESS AND EMOTIONAL HYGIENE – A USEFUL CHECKLIST

Emotional hygiene is a term often used now to describe a way of managing the essential factors that contribute to a balanced, healthy lifestyle that we need in order to function well. Both scientific evidence and common sense point to a basic list of *dos* and *don'ts* if we want to give ourselves the best chance of remaining emotionally stable and sufficiently resourceful to deal with the stresses and crises that are a regular part of life.

There is nothing new or magical in this approach. A healthy mind and body are better able to respond appropriately in times of crisis. If we are tired (it has been estimated that 30 per cent of us don't get enough sleep), smoke and/or drink too much, lack social support or in any other way feel alienated from society, are not being stretched in our work and/or play, we are likely to be less healthy than we would otherwise be, to the detriment of our coping ability.

We are bombarded these days with advice on how to live our lives. Much of the time we would rather ignore it, whether it comes from 'experts' in the media or from people closer to us, for each of us feels we know better than anyone else what is best for us. Yet the changes which are usually necessary to enhance our sense of well-being are relatively small ones. They all involve the human givens, the needs nature programmed into us. Check the list below and see for yourself whether your routine could be improved to develop greater emotional hygiene.

## Do you:

**Get enough sleep?** YES SOMETIMES NO

People now sleep, on average, 500 hours less per year than they did ninety years ago – a loss of 20 per cent. Research shows that a reduction in sleep time of only 10 per cent can have a negative effect on how we think and behave. If you often wake up tired and find it difficult to motivate yourself, you are worrying excessively and vulnerable to depression.

**Exercise regularly?** YES SOMETIMES NO

Regular exercise (fifteen to thirty minutes at least three times a week) is important for what it does to the mind, as well as the body. Furthermore, some sort of routine has benefits apart from those related directly to the physical and mental aspects of our lives; we programme in time for ourselves, become absorbed in whatever exercise we have chosen and, if we join a club or group, make social contact. Exercise does not have to be vigorous, sustained or extreme. A daily, brisk walk, enough to make the heart pound faster, say the experts, is all most of us need.

**Eat sensibly and appropriately?** YES SOMETIMES NO

There is no shortage of advice on what constitutes a healthy and balanced diet. What we eat of course also affects mind and body, but one aspect that is often ignored is how and where we eat. It is important not to rush. Meals should be eaten unhurriedly while sitting at a table, preferably in company we enjoy. This is emotionally healthier (and better for the digestion) than grabbing a snack while standing on a railway platform or in a burger bar. Generally we are allowing less and less time for eating.

EMOTIONAL HYGIENE ◂

**Monitor negative 'self-talk'?** YES SOMETIMES NO
We all have negative thoughts that cross our minds. Don't
let these go unchallenged. These very often reflect negative
beliefs we have about ourselves, others or life in general that
have been conditioned into us. Beware they don't act like self-
administered post-hypnotic suggestions and become self-
fulfilling prophecies.

**Smoke and/or drink?** YES SOMETIMES NO
Nothing new here. If you must do it, do it in moderation.
Ideally you should follow the health guidelines for alcohol
consumption and not smoke at all.

**Get enough privacy?** YES SOMETIMES NO
Time to ourselves, such as regular involvement with a hobby
or interest or reading, has known benefits. For one thing,
it forces us to 'switch off' from our daily cares and concerns.
Also, to be involved in a project we enjoy means that we
will be drawn to the activity (because we are enjoying it)
rather than having to force ourselves to get up and get
on with something. Even within families and close
partnerships it is important to find your own space.

**Enjoy social interaction?** YES SOMETIMES NO
We all need to be involved in something greater than
ourselves to draw us out of a narrow concern with ourselves.
This could mean doing things for a local pressure group or
PTA, a church, a charity, looking after other people or animals,
working for a political movement, a football club or joining
a choir or theatre group. The essential thing is to have an
unselfish sense of commitment to the wider community.

**Have social support?** YES SOMETIMES NO
Do you have friends with whom you can discuss things if you
need to? This does not necessarily mean in the deep, 'heart-
to-heart' sense, but we need a sense of connectedness with
those around us, and, if things go wrong at work, or in the
family, it is useful to know other people we can compare
notes with outside the place where the trouble is occurring.

**Laugh a lot?** YES SOMETIMES NO
Laughter is one of the great de-stressors and is best done
in company.

**Have projects that stretch you?** YES SOMETIMES NO
Are you involved in or looking forward to something you
are planning coming to fruition? Do you have realisable
plans or ambitions? We function better when we have a
sense of scale and achievement in our lives.

**Manage your busy days?** YES SOMETIMES NO
This means planning a schedule that you manage, rather
than one which manages you, and allowing time to do things
and delegating efficiently where possible. If you lead a busy
life this is essential to prevent being overwhelmed.

**Always feel prepared for change?** YES SOMETIMES NO
The mentally healthiest people know that we live a transient
life and none of us can be certain that we will be alive
tomorrow. They regard change as the only stable factor in life
and thereby do not automatically see change as a threat with
negative consequences. When the unexpected happens they
don't suffer from unnecessary stress symptoms and the
resultant mental instability and physical health problems.

**Use stress-management techniques?** YES SOMETIMES NO
There are many ways to bring down arousal levels and
achieve a therapeutic state of deep relaxation. These
essentially mean making time for yourself in private and
include: visualisation techniques, breathing out more
slowly than you breathe in, gentle massage, aromatherapy,
listening to relaxing music, getting away to somewhere
beautiful and walking, swimming etc.

**Have intimacy in your life?** YES SOMETIMES NO
Everyone needs at least one person with whom they can
be totally themselves and know they are accepted for who
they are.

**Have physical contact?** YES SOMETIMES NO
Touch is important to us. Do you have regular, pleasant
physical contact with the special person or people in your life?

**Give and receive enough attention?** YES SOMETIMES NO
Attention is best seen as a type of nutrition. When we get
too little attention we become starved of it and crave it.
Too much and we become bloated with self-importance
and addicted to it. As with food, it should be of a good quality
and exchanged in a balanced way. And we can do with less
of it than we usually desire! All human interactions become
easier to understand when you can see the attention
component in them. Giving good-quality attention
to others is a human duty.

**Self-regulate?** YES SOMETIMES NO
If you are happy with the answers you have given to the
questions above, and think that your emotional needs are
being met, you need to have a way to make sure you can spot
if anything starts to go off-balance. For example, you could
refer to this list from time to time and see how you are doing.

# chapter 3
# STATUS – be careful what you strive for

## NICK'S STORY

One of the earliest emotions I remember was that of needing to do better than my parents. It was instilled in me at an early age by my mother constantly telling me that she wanted me to do better than she had. Very quickly it became a mantra that needed to be adopted to achieve favour with her.

Ours was a working-class family. My father was a plasterer who didn't really have any interest in reading, other than the tabloids, and then principally from the back forwards. His income wasn't sufficient to maintain the whole family. He grew up playing football, and that's all he wanted to do. I was certainly closer to my mother. She was a strong character who wore the trousers in the house and who encouraged me in everything. Most of the time she looked after us kids – me, my brother Richard and my sisters Victoria and Sarah – and that would be her primary role during the day. She did a bit of nursing, mostly night work, but she wasn't always employed. As far as I can remember, her view of society was structured into the traditional hierarchy of working, middle and upper classes. She wanted us all to aspire to the next level on the social ladder. Jobs in accountancy, banking or the law characterised the ideal that she had set in her mind for her children's careers. I seem to have touched on all of them in one way or another but, as far as the latter is concerned, certainly not in the way she would have wished.

Dad used to like the horses so she made sure she looked after the money. She did the shopping, paid the bills and made sure we had everything we needed. So she was exceptionally hard working in those roles, but she wanted her children to achieve more than she had. She valued learning and saw it as a way to a better life.

I liked to win. I liked the praise and the status that was associated with it. Whether I was playing football, running a cross-country race or taking a maths test, I had a massive hunger to be first. I certainly wasn't the most gifted footballer or runner but it was important for me to be part of the team, part of the in-crowd, to be accepted as an equal among people who were clearly a little better. It was a tall order, a target that was unrealistic, but one that I blundered towards on a daily basis.

Looking back on my life, it's fascinating how much role-playing there has been. I think this started when I was at school. The schools I attended were staunchly middle class, and we would have been one of the poorer families there. My mother would always make sure we had what we needed so that we didn't feel any different – the latest football boots, a new bike etc. – but by the age of eleven the difference in privilege between the other kids and myself was painfully obvious.

The role-playing certainly continued during my working life. I became part of the banking fraternity, doing well and advancing through the ranks. I have always been socially adept, able to mix in any number of groups, but that is little more than role-playing. My whole time in Singapore was spent playing a role – at work, or at home with my first wife. Nobody knew what was going on and I was the last person who would be able to tell them.

At school I was academically sound. Through junior school I was always at the top of the class, though I don't really remember much about it, other than playing kiss-chase and things like that. By the time I left at the age of eleven I was probably a year ahead of everybody else in terms of reading and numeracy. That was down to my mum's help, always wanting me to achieve. She was the one who would sit with me, help me understand the schoolwork and encourage me to read the books. That stress to achieve was ever present throughout my childhood, and I think it probably dawned on me when I was about fifteen how unrealistic my targets were, and that I would have to settle for something lower. I suppose I rebelled a little around that period, scraping myself through all of the classes and cramming around the exam periods to make sure I had something to fall back on. For a while I suppose I wanted to belong more than I wanted to achieve. And I'm not sure which one of those has potentially the more damaging side-effects when those needs are not met.

Dad kept out of my academic learning totally. Maybe he had no interest but, looking back, I think it was more because it was an area of life where he may have floundered a bit. I can't actually remember one episode where he sat down and helped me with my homework. He wasn't a great speller, so it was probably beyond his experience and capabilities to help me academically. I'm not too different from him in some of the ways that I deal and have dealt with tricky situations in my life. I'll avoid them rather than bring any inadequacies crashing into the open and be embarrassed by the fall-out. I try to please everybody; and that obviously isn't possible and it sometimes gets me into scrapes where being honest would cause more problems than it would solve. I would fear that admitting my lack of knowledge, admitting an inability to sort something out, would damage the status I had in the relationship. I fed the managers and directors of Barings a complete 'cock and bull' story for three long years. It seems to me that they all swallowed it, individually and collectively. The only reason I can find to explain the ease with which they swallowed it is that they might not have wanted to highlight their own lack of knowledge by asking questions.

I would say my relationship with my father has always been sound if somewhat distant. It shifted when my mother died, but I was only twenty then. I would have handled things differently to him, but we all grieve differently. Dad and I are still fairly close, but not as close as we were. I'm still basically the same person I was back then. I haven't changed much.

It was my mother who pushed me through school, and to this day I can't get rid of the motivating force she instilled in me. My need to achieve somehow overpowered me and ultimately led to the collapse of a 200-year-old merchant bank. That need never seemed to have had any natural or imposed limits, and I'm very conscious now of the need to temper my needs and desires and be content more readily. There were episodes during my life where the need to be stretched was adequately met, but I still wanted more. I became overambitious and hungry for status. And that could be where it became damaging.

## IN CONVERSATION

**IVAN**

Nick, I'd like to pick up on one thing, first of all: you say you haven't changed much. That just doesn't ring true.

**NICK**

Why not?

**IVAN**

Well, we all come with a history. We all have a special relationship with our parents, hopefully both of them, and we all have things that happen to us at school as we grow up and go out to work. What's really interesting about your story is that in addition to your upbringing you had some very unusual life experiences – ones the whole world knows about. The continual stress over those years almost certainly was a major factor in why you got seriously ill. You had to endure a major operation in prison, yet you survived, came out and rebuilt your life. It's just not possible to remain unchanged by all that. You learned *something*. We've just got to find out what. I believe an unusual life like yours can help us see how amazing human resilience really is.

**NICK**

When you put it like that … yes, I *have* learned. For example, knowing I came through all of those events gives me an inner strength I know I can draw on when needed.

**IVAN**

It is life's difficulties that show us who and what we are.

## NICK

I'm not an exceptionally brave person; twelve years ago I would have been hard pushed to imagine coping with any of the things that have happened to me over the intervening years. But I had to cope; I had no choice. I was in the situation and had to deal with it, so that was what I did – poorly as regards my career at Barings but, to a degree, more successfully in everything that happened to me thereafter. With anything that happens to me now, however potentially damaging, frightening or difficult it is, there is the inner strength or ability to overcome it. I know how strong I can be when required. Nothing much these days either frightens me or causes me too much stress. That's not to say that I wouldn't get stressed out about the most ordinary thing, because I do. Money is an example of something I do still worry about. I owe the liquidators £100 million, so I'm not really starting from a very solid base. I have a family to look after and I'm conscious of the fact that, with my record, I'm not the most employable person in the world. So I always have one eye on the future in respect of financial matters. I'm clearly not stress-free but I do feel better equipped now than I ever have been in the past. If I'm driving down the road and someone suddenly pulls out in front of me, I don't get irate and rant and rave any more. Before my time in prison I would have done. I've been in so many situations in the last few years where I couldn't possibly impact on what was happening around me, prison being the most obvious example. I can't influence an idiot's driving patterns, so I just make sure that I keep myself safe and let him get on with it. It may be a simple philosophy but it works. Rather than applying myself too much to problem-solving, now I tend to look for the simplest solution and stick with that. Looking back at the Barings fiasco it's easy to see that I had many opportunities to do things differently, so that I would not have gone to prison. For example, I could have stopped trading at any time; I could have gone to the management and told them of the losses far, far earlier, and Barings would have recovered. But I never did. Something – a force almost – stopped me. So maybe I *have* changed because I know I wouldn't make the same mistake now. My demise is a huge embarrassment to me, one that never diminishes. There were things I could have done differently, that I could have controlled, theoretically, but I never did.

**IVAN**

The really interesting thing is, why?

**NICK**

That is probably the thing I find hardest to put my finger on. I had so many chances to change direction, virtually every day, and I ignored them all, which was irrational in the extreme. I only had to pick up the phone or walk round the corner to someone's office and let them know what was going on. It couldn't have been simpler. There were many times when I played golf with the Managing Director and I'd hate myself throughout the eighteen holes. I wouldn't be able to look him in the eye in case he saw all the deceit that was hiding behind mine. I wanted nothing more than to put it right and start again. That was my dream. But telling everyone, anyone, what was going wrong, was my worst possible nightmare.

## IVAN

The force that stopped you from saying things were going wrong was a human given: the need for status. We are driven to sense our status level within the different groups we live and work with. And, particularly when we are young and trying to establish ourselves in the world, we try to raise our status. The higher the status, the generally more secure we feel. It's a consequence of our having evolved as social creatures. Someone put in a position of importance in an organisation, like you were, has status, more than employees under you, but not as much as those over you. You are halfway up the greasy pole. You have to project competence and always appear on top of your operation, even when inside you know you are not. To the outside world, for two or three years or so, you seemed to be doing incredibly well. It was inevitable that, once you had that status of being a dynamic young trader, making lots of money for Barings in the Far East, you couldn't let it go. The need for status is a powerful drive, especially when you are a young, testosterone-fuelled man. It would be going against nature to ignore that. It's very hard to admit that things are going horribly wrong because you've made big mistakes. To do so requires rising above nature, and only exceptional people can do that. This primitive fear of loss of status is why people in positions of power find it so difficult to admit mistakes. It's no different from what often happens when a child is learning to ride a bike and falls off and hurts itself. When it sees people smiling knowingly at it, it often truculently says, 'I *meant* to do that!'

## NICK

Until I read your book I always thought the word for this was 'pride'. I just hadn't thought it through. Status is not a word I would have subscribed to but now I think it's very valid. It explains so much. Obviously at Barings there were people around me who played a peripheral role in supporting my sense of status, and I would have reciprocated it. These were the people that worked for me in the same environment, those at a similar level within the organisation, and those at a superior level for whom I worked. The status of everyone was being reinforced all the time. Now I think about it, it may be the case that status was also a factor with my then wife, Lisa. She seemed to me to be very much caught up in my role within Barings and how much I was succeeding. Maybe it was a status thing for her too. Until now though, I always viewed it as not wanting to let any of those people down. I thought it was pride, and didn't see the connection with the need for status. But sitting with you here now it does make sense. I desperately didn't want to lose that status among all the people around me. It made me feel good, too, even if it was based on a pack of lies. I was the talk of the trading floor every day; every time somebody traded with me they lost money. I'd stand tall and defiant, foolishly take on the market, force the markets temporarily higher and project the image of a winner; the image of success. As I singed the hands of some of the locals that traded with me in Singapore, my position in Tokyo was like a bush fire that was spreading out of control.

**IVAN**

I'm sure that's right. It's a given that we have different status within different groups – the domestic family, our neighbours, our peer group and friends, our colleagues at work, our business clients etc. This status is a form of security. It doesn't even mean being at the top. We all just need to know we have status at some meaningful level and are accepted. A further complication is that males and females get their status needs met in different ways.

## STATUS – HOW MEN AND WOMEN DIFFER

Men and women are seldom more equal than in their lack of understanding of one another. When pointing out behavioural differences between the sexes, one attempts to summarise the results of tens of thousands of research studies from around the world about the common, average differences between men and women. There are always exceptions: some heterosexual men are more masculine than others and some heterosexual women are more feminine than others. Some men have a more feminine way of thinking and reacting and some women have a more masculine approach to thinking and problem-solving than most women. But in general:

▸ Men respond to systems and symbols in the external world. They 'salute the rank, not the person'. Men talk to give information or to report on events and establish their status. They talk about *things* – cars,

work, politics, ideas, research, sport, food, drink –
rather than people. They are more interested in
conveying facts, not emotional responses. They
mistrust emotions. They are goal-oriented. They
focus on solving problems and find it more productive
to concentrate on one task at a time. They are less
likely to ask for help or directions. Men compete.

► Women respond to emotional connections to people.
A woman has high status among other women
if she knows a lot about people's relationships.
Women talk to get information and to get into
rapport and connect with other people. For women,
how well they do this determines their status.
They talk about people rather than things. They
trust emotions and convey feelings and details and
are relationship-oriented. Who they know and what
they know about other people is more interesting
to them than statistics. They are better at multi-
tasking and quicker to ask for, and accept, help or
directions. Women co-operate.

HOW MEN AND WOMEN DIFFER ◄

**NICK**

I agree entirely. There's a hierarchy in this. I could not
bring myself to run away and disappear into anonymity.
That would have been impossible. I held on to my position at the bank, my status, until the last possible
moment. When I finally did run away it was absolutely at

the last moment. The relationships I had at work were not at the top of my 'fear of losing status' list. Even more important was my status in the domestic situation: with my wife and family. My real friends were not quite so high on the list because they would remain my friends afterwards, whatever I did. Further down the hierarchy were colleagues and then clients. With hindsight, I can see the hierarchy. Just as I didn't want to let my wife and myself down, I also didn't want to let my seniors in Singapore down. They were exceptionally nice people who did whatever they could for me. I felt that if they found out what I was doing it would be like throwing their kindness back in their faces. As I worked I was trying to repay their faith and trust properly, but didn't – which is a complicated thing to describe. They did have superior status to me; they had achieved what I would have liked to achieve. But I was too proud to ask for help when I was in difficulty. Just going to the Managing Director, for instance, and exposing the web of lies I had created was a step I couldn't take. I couldn't face him and say that all this profit they thought I was making was a lie, and demean myself by asking for help. That's one of the biggest failings I had at the time. Consequently I'm very conscious of it now. If I can't cope with something today, or I'm troubled in some way, I *will* ask for help. That's a key change in me.

## IVAN

Most of us change as we get older and become less self-conscious. Young people are more driven by the need for status while they are establishing themselves in the world.

Your youth plus the absurdity of gambling with hundreds of millions of pounds of other people's money were a heady mix.

## NICK

The point about my youth is valid, but the one about gambling isn't. In banking it is considered legitimate to gamble with other people's money. It was, and is, a normal function of the market. I never thought about what would happen to other people if it went wrong. And I never expected the bank to collapse. If there had been a dramatic rogue-trading escapade that I had known about prior to my own, perhaps the knowledge of some of the consequences would have curbed much of my calamitous decision making. My story should serve as a warning for anyone entering the financial market. I knew there would be substantial losses, but quite how dramatic the consequences of my actions were came as much of a surprise to me as everyone else. Small comfort I suppose. Looking back I can see my need for status was met at home and in school. I did well at junior school and at senior school I got good O and A levels. When I was eighteen my mother pushed me to get a good job and helped me apply for a position in the City, at Coutts. So from leaving school I progressed very rapidly. By the time I was twenty I had moved to Morgan Stanley and was earning £20,000 a year – a fortune compared to what some of my Watford friends were earning. I bought my first flat then. I had status all right! It's strange but as soon as I started work I began living two separate lives. There was my job and working role, and there was my home life and fun-time-socialising role. I kept them very much apart. To a degree that's what allowed me to succeed so well in the banking world for as long as I did. I could totally focus on whatever I was doing because there was little interplay between the two roles. The role-playing had started very early in my life. Coming from a working-class background and going to a middle-class school, and wanting to fit in with the other kids, involved me role-playing being middle class. Then, going into the business-banking world also involved a degree of role-playing. I didn't necessarily like the people I worked with but I loved the job. It was always the job that excited and stretched me. I was never made to feel confined in what I could do. I'm not speaking from experience, because I haven't done them, but I think there are certain jobs where you reach a point where it doesn't stretch you any more, and it becomes drudgery. That must be stressful. I never felt that.

### IVAN

Being stretched is definitely what makes people feel alive and gives meaning to existence. But even the most ordinary work can do that if one does it with full attention, especially when other people value what you are doing.

### NICK

Of course. I'm not wishing to downplay any other type of work but I'm sure there are a lot of people who will read this book who feel stuck in their working life and find it pretty much meaningless drudgery. And that's because their work doesn't stretch them. There must be ways they can refocus the way they look at their role in the organisation and have their status needs met.

**IVAN**

You're right. The fragile mental health of much of the population stems from this problem: if people's brains are not stretched, they degenerate.

**NICK**

I suppose they are stressed because they are not being stretched. I changed jobs fairly frequently during my working life. I needed to – as soon as the tasks became repetitive, mundane or lacking in challenge I needed to move on. The challenges at Coutts and Company and Morgan Stanley dried up after a couple of years. My needs had outgrown the organisation. Lucky for them!

**IVAN**

There's a huge difference between being *stressed* and being *stretched*. If children are not stretched with challenges, they don't fulfil their potential. They will always feel, deep down, that something is missing from their lives. An engine has to be looked after and driven or it rusts away. The brain is no different. And that law applies right up until we die. We can't escape the need to keep stretching ourselves without paying a terrible price. Stress, by contrast, is where you feel that you have no control over what's happening. Your body produces stress hormones, but you are not burning them off in productive, useful ways by stretching yourself and getting back in control. That's the cause of stress-induced problems, like anxiety, anger and depression and all the physical symptoms of stress. A lot of people are stressed just through boredom and the feeling that they have no real control over their lives and the type of work they do. They try to compensate by entertaining themselves in various ways, but if it's passive entertainment that doesn't stretch them, like watching too much TV or doing drugs or drink, ultimately their lives become substandard.

**NICK**

It would be so good if people could grasp that: that if you're not stretching yourself you are more susceptible to stress. It is a profound bit of knowledge.

**IVAN**

It's something many people aren't aware of.

**NICK**

Yes, but it's key. And I suppose, to a degree, if you're not being stretched through your role in an organisation or the work you do, you have to look for it in other ways.

**IVAN**

You have to try to build it into other areas of your life. You have to change your attitude to the boring work because, if being in a job just to earn money makes you feel resentful, that's raising stress levels. But if you say to yourself, OK, it's not ideal, but I'm producing money for my family so we have a roof over our heads and we can all eat, and I can have spare time to pursue what I really want to do in the evenings and at weekends, the work then becomes more meaningful. It's always the perception and attitude of the person that determines how stressed they are.

**NICK**

It's the mindset. Whether or not you believe you can influence the things that are happening around you, the one thing you can most definitely influence is the way you think about them.

**IVAN**

You can have two people in an identical situation, say, dying of cancer: one is stressed out and depressed and the other is still getting as much out of life as possible. It's summed up in that old phrase 'Two people looked out through prison bars, one saw mud and the other saw stars.' It's what you focus on that counts.

**NICK**

I learned that in prison. It's an important message I want people to understand. Whatever unfortunate position you find yourself in, you've just got to reappraise it and come at it from a different angle.

**IVAN**

It's what psychotherapists call 'reframing'.

**NICK**

I've had to do it time and time again in varying degrees of difficulty and sometimes the more abstract you can be in your thinking the better. We all have positives in our lives but they're not always the easiest to see. When I was diagnosed with cancer, as frightening as the disease was, I had a chance; there were actions I could undertake to increase my chances of survival. A lot of people I know are in situations that bring them down: lousy relationships, being ill, being addicted to something, or not wanting to go to work on a Monday. They probably need to do some 'reframing'.

## IVAN

Well, rates of depression are on a huge upswing statistically and I think this is mainly because our society has the technology to create massive amounts of unrealistic expectations in us. TV, computer games and the Internet, though wonderful, can be dangerous because the brain actually works through *expectations* – and expectations can be manipulated by a bombardment of messages about where you are on the status hierarchy. If you create a society that engenders a large number of unrealistic expectations in its members, you are actually making people more vulnerable and working against evolution. This is because evolution is about *refining* expectations to better ensure survival. People are exposed to a continual diet of high-emotion, action-packed drama, but you never ever see superheroes or celebrities spending hours filling out insurance forms or having to endure the day-to-day ordinary but stressful banalities, such as commuting. Or we listen to pop songs that sing of either perfect love or, at the other extreme, self-aggrandizing lust. This affects our expectations too. And millions watch soap operas that implicitly make people expect that family life should involve lots of emoting and sentimentality. This reduces our tolerance for the essential but more mundane activities that actually glue families together. If people come to expect that their work should be full of drama and excitement, or that relationships should be either 'perfect', whatever that is, or involve lots of shouting and screaming, because that's what actors are doing on television, they are bound to feel bad. Our society doesn't yet have a handle on the fact that strong emotions, except where they are needed for survival, make us less than human – stupid, even, because they actually inhibit the function of our higher cortex.

## NICK

There's been a definite shift in me regards my expectations of work since I was released from prison. Fortunately bits of work and money just seemed to come in. I've been doing some after-dinner speaking and I write a couple of columns for magazines – piecemeal stuff that doesn't take up too many hours or stretch me much. But, since remarrying, taking on two stepchildren, now having a baby, I am more conscious that I need a reliable income. I'd like to do something again that stretched me every day, similar to the way I was stretched in the banks I worked for, where I was always learning new things and rising to challenges. That's what I really enjoyed about work and what I want now. Having spoken to you for the last few hours I'm certainly worried about what that lack of stretching may lead to, what it may degenerate into. Obviously I'm acutely aware that a bank wouldn't take me on after what I did. But I *have* changed. My mindset is different. For one thing I'm conscious that I need to be stretched and I need to put money on the table. That would remove a major stress factor for me, one that doesn't really have to be there. I'm sure the same is true for everyone.

### IVAN

The absolute biological necessity of being stretched fascinates me, too. Some of the hardest people to treat in therapy are the sons and daughters of parents who are wealthy enough to support their grown-up children so they never have to work hard, never have to struggle. It makes no difference how 'clever' they are, whether they have a good degree or not. They often end up living at home in their thirties; they lose sight of the point of anything and become cynical and depressed. They may *pretend* to work – by dabbling in the arts or 'investigating Buddhism' – but they are not actually doing anything that really stretches them because there is no bottom line; Mummy and Daddy will bail them out. They fall apart because they don't *have* to do anything. Just like the lost souls on long-term state benefits, they are not using their innate resources to stretch themselves. They just rot like rubber bands that have lost their elasticity.

### NICK

I have met people like that. But there are people on the dole who really don't like it. Single mums who want to work but have to live off benefits because the way the system is structured in the UK means that if you do go out to work and stretch yourself you are less well off financially than drawing benefit. So people deliberately repress that need to stretch themselves, which again is extremely unhealthy. If there was a way to bring that gap a little bit closer to enable people to stop repressing that need to stretch themselves, that would be one of the best things that a government could ever do. It would give people back self-esteem. Unfortunately I don't think that it will ever happen; the structures are too embedded.

**IVAN**

Let's talk about self-esteem. They say pride comes before a fall. You had a big fall.

**NICK**

I must have had a lot of pride! My self-esteem took a bit of a knock. I had a lot of time to reflect on it while I was in prison. I looked at myself and reflected on how I had been and what I had become. To be honest, I didn't like what I saw.

**IVAN**

Well, we need to unpack such words as pride and self-esteem. We've already said that pride is connected with the need for status. But what does pride *really* mean? Parents can be proud of their child doing well. A gardener can take pride in his beautiful garden. It's the carrot we all need to feel good about things. In unnaturally high-stress, target-oriented environments like you worked in, people can come to think that self-worth is measured by how well they achieve the targets and, if they don't come up to scratch, they can begin to feel like a failure, harshly judged by their peers, bosses and society in general. Low self-esteem, which means really believing you are rubbish, is an awful thing. But the idea that the opposite of low self-esteem is high self-esteem, and that high self-esteem is a good thing, is not accurate. The wisest people of all ages and all cultures have viewed 'esteeming the self' as unhealthy. Competent people who have a generally positive attitude to life and to themselves on average are healthier and live longer. It would be quite wrong, however, to describe such people as 'having high self-esteem'. It's easy to see why when we look at the five characteristics of high self-esteem:

- self-satisfied boasting
- smugness
- abusing power relationships (by automatically assuming their wants are paramount in any situation)
- adopting an air of assumed superiority (just because they have competence or good fortune in a particular area of life)
- being blind to their own faults

People who are 'full of self-esteem' actually tend to behave like psychopaths. What is popularly called 'low self-esteem', by contrast, is associated with pessimism, depression and withdrawing from life, and is therefore unhealthy. People can be conditioned by abusive parents, teachers and employers to believe they are useless. After such conditioning they would certainly be undervaluing and understating their ability to get their needs met, which stops them learning the necessary skills to do so. The way to get people to feel OK about themselves is to encourage competence. This is because, unless a person feels that they are being recognised for their competence, and feel that they are achieving something, they'll never flourish. They'll languish like a drought-stricken tree. The whole of society seems to have become obsessed with management by targets. This is autistic, 'straight-line' thinking and causes chaos. Obviously goals have to be set and results have to be measured. As a money man you more than anyone know things have to add up, and when they don't things go wrong. But when complex operations neglect basic needs and become blindly target-driven it can override the very purpose of the organisation. One only has to look at the stress-levels of teachers and those working in the medical profession: meeting targets has been prioritised over the nature of the job itself. Using targets is a very one-dimensional approach to making things run smoothly. This straight-line thinking occurs in the financial world as well, doesn't it?

**NICK**

Very much so. But I now think that setting targets is a zero-sum game. They set people up to compete against their peers in other organisations and everyone always want to be associated with the organisation making the most money, having the most success in the industry. The key players in any bank have the most power in their own organisation but also among their peers in other banks. They are also the most likely to jump ship for a better offer. Loyalty counts for nothing. This money-determined pecking order filters down through each level in each organisation. So everyone in the trading environment is trying to make as much money as they can. Those who are most visibly 'making the money' are the obvious key players. This diminishes the status of those working in the equally important support roles of the business. Despite their vital roles they never get to share in the huge salaries and bonuses the traders get. All the banking scandals seemed to involve both the drive to meet and exceed targets and weaknesses in the back office, the support functions. This seemed to be the case in the recent Allied Irish Bank rogue-trading scandal in Baltimore with their subsidiary All First and again at the National Australia Bank in Melbourne. The ubiquitous minor scandals involving banks regularly overcharging customers occur because back-office roles don't make money – they cost money, and reduce bank revenues. Therefore banks don't pay too much attention to them. They can easily withstand the losses that ensue because they make billions of pounds a year by focusing on trading – making money out of money.

A bank in Ireland was exposed recently for overcharging for foreign exchange transactions to the tune of €30 million. They had to pay a goodwill deposit of the same amount to the Central Bank. You would imagine that it would be quite damaging to the bank but it wasn't in the slightest. It takes them two days to make an income of €60 million; pocket change when you think of what they had been getting away with prior to that. That type of greed-based business environment creates all kinds of problems. Everybody is trying to make as much money as they possibly can in order to gain that status. Their self-esteem is related to highly visible signs of material success. I have to say that it suited my personality, too, at the time.

**IVAN**

Feeling good about yourself comes from feeling competent and achieving things.

**NICK**

That's it exactly.

**IVAN**

But that doesn't mean that you have to 'esteem' yourself and believe you are wonderful.

**NICK**

I think competence is the word. Rather than internalising that competence, I wanted to show it in the most obvious way I could and to as many people as possible. Perhaps it was ego but I wanted my ability recognised. I always thought I was better able to do a job or fulfil a task more easily than anyone else: being competent was never enough for me; I wanted to be the best.

**IVAN**

Did you feel that even your best was never good enough, for your mother, for instance?

**NICK**

No, not at all. Until the age of eleven I couldn't have been any better. I was *the* best. At that age there was a very clear, results-based standard that placed me in a hierarchy of achievement in terms of my fellow pupils. I was always several levels ahead of my classmates. O and A levels had a broader grading standard where the differentiation was not so clear. The financial markets propelled me back into an environment where it was easy to judge who was top dog, who was best. Perhaps that need to be the best resurfaced there.

**IVAN**

So you could never settle for just being competent?

**NICK**

Settling for competence could potentially have changed my whole life story. As soon as I was at the top of the class, when I was a kid, I was competent in my mother's eyes. And I took that feeling into Coutts, Morgan Stanley and Barings. I was always one of the brightest employees and progressed well. It was a competitive environment where you gauged yourself against the people around you, and I wanted to advance to the top. But that need to be number one is probably not realistic because there are thousands trying to be number one and we can't all reach the pinnacle.

**IVAN**

That's absolutely right. This will become more meaningful to you as your son grows up. At school children are good at different things. To be obsessed at measuring a few markers, like basic literacy and numeracy, is not realistic because people can become competent in the most obscure subjects, and achieve in the most unexpected ways. Children who are seen as real dunces at school can turn out to be geniuses at propagating plants or navigation. Individual talent often operates outside of a rigid school curriculum.

**NICK**

Some of the most successful people I've known were never academically that bright. And yet they've done fantastically well in business. I think there's been a mood change though. When I was growing up in the mid to late seventies, those targets my mother set me at the time – to be top – were too high. People now are more realistic about the targets they set their children; they think those targets were too high and achieving them not so important. Perhaps my generation was the last to really see that and was totally turned off by the way it was manifested in their lives. I see that more and more. My friends all have children. My sister has children. I have stepchildren and a child of my own now. Everybody wants their children to do well in school, but they don't seem to want to push them as hard as I was pushed. The need to achieve and do better has been softened somewhat over the generations.

**IVAN**

What actually happens when somebody really gets interested in something is that they are 'pulled', not 'pushed'. A brilliant teacher can get children engaged in a topic for hours a day, every day. Children can master a language in a month if they feel pulled to do so. They love it. And that applies to most subjects. They need to feel with everything they learn that their competence is growing.

**NICK**

I know everything exists on a continuum but do you think my desire for status, and stretching myself to achieve it, became unhealthy?

**IVAN**

It's a very interesting question. In our psychologically unsophisticated culture the notion that our essential needs have to be met in a balanced way is not commonly understood. Not even by professionals who you might think should understand, like teachers, social workers or psychotherapists. Wherever you find lopsided behaviour it signifies a combination of *unmet needs* or *conditioned greediness*. When a person becomes greedy, whether for attention, control, status or to be emotionally connected to others, it stops them seeing their true condition. It colours their view of everyone around them and narrows down their options. One meets status-obsessed people who think, for example, that someone who doesn't have as much money as they do or doesn't own such a large house or drive such a good car is not worth talking to. But some of the most amazing individuals are those for whom possessions mean little.

## NICK

Perhaps at Barings I was blinded by the status I aspired to and that stopped me thinking through the consequences of what I was doing. It makes sense. However bad it got, I always managed to think I had some control over the situation; that I would be able to trade myself into profit and walk away from the self-made hell. It never happened; it was highly unlikely when it would ever happen, but I held on to that belief for as long as I possibly could. There were many times that I feared the next knock on the door but there were also times when the confidence was high, bolstered by positions that were doing well and a lack of questions from London. Occasionally I was almost carefree.

## IVAN

A lot of people will identify with that. Greed is a strong emotion. From the moment we're born we all need attention –

as we've said, it's a form of nutrition. Without attention our brains don't develop properly. So, if we are starved of attention, we can become needy and greedy for it. But being given too much attention or status can be just as harmful. It's the same kind of relationship we have with food. It harms us to starve and it harms us to overeat. It's always a question of balance and timing.

**NICK**

My baby's a couple of months old. If we pick him up all the time and constantly give him a huge amount of attention, won't he start to think that he is the centre of the universe?

**IVAN**

From his point of view he *is* the centre of the universe. He has to be because his safety and survival depend on you and Leona. He would die if left alone. Every infant, for the first three or four years, has to regard his needs as paramount and the rest of the universe is secondary. Every child starts life feeling like that, but then, gradually, it should be weaned off that feeling and helped to learn how to delay gratification and recognise that other people have needs and have to be given attention and have their needs satisfied too. If a child is brought up well, that's what happens. But unfortunately not all children grow up in healthy environments. You see many damaged adolescents and adults who believe that every whim, desire and greed they feel has to be satisfied immediately, as of right. They are stuck in a typical two-year-old's attention-seeking behaviour, probably because they were not given an appropriate amount of attention in their early years. And our propensity to be greedy as a society is also destroying the environment that sustains us.

**NICK**

I agree. We need to develop competence at looking after the planet. With hindsight, up until the age of 25 when I moved to Singapore, I did feel extremely competent. Everything I'd been asked to do I'd been able to do. I overcame every challenge, usually with something to spare. But in Singapore, when the error trading account on the Singapore International Monetary Exchange (SIMEX) was opened, I quickly began to feel incompetent. Rather than admit to the feeling that I couldn't cope, I bottled it up and tried to bluff it out. Rationality went out the window!

**IVAN**

Was that when the real stress started?

**NICK**

Yes.

**IVAN**

Can you remember the moment when you suddenly realised you were out of your depth? Was there a dawning awareness, for example, that you were telling lies to cover up mistakes? Did you feel a tightening in your chest or an unpleasant feeling in your stomach as you thought, Oh God, I shouldn't have done that?

**NICK**

Well, yes. I had the butterflies in the stomach and feelings of panic spreading through me. But it wasn't until late in the evening that we realised we had the error – close to midnight. The trade ended up in the 88888 account. Placing the position in that account was the riskiest thing I had ever done. I had complete autonomy; it was a test of my basic integrity and I failed. Sure, if it had worked, no one would have been any the wiser and my life would have been completely different. There is something to be said for efficient and rigorous control mechanisms. I knew what I was doing was wrong and I knew I shouldn't be doing it, but I continued all the same. When I first moved to Singapore I was very much an outsider in the local office. I was fighting for every bit of status I could get. The day started at seven o'clock, and the computer systems we had to settle trades weren't the best. In an ideal world, or any normal functioning market, if I were to do a trade with someone, it would be confirmed within a half-hour period. But the computers would often crash for four or five hours at a time, so there was a lot of exposure that was obviously cause for concern. We couldn't match those trades.

**IVAN**

Computers weren't as good then as they are now.

**NICK**

To a degree. What aggravated the situation was that, whereas the SIMEX market used to do two thousand contracts a day, with our arrival, and one or two other companies joining in, it quickly went up to twenty thousand a day. The system couldn't cope. The computers were stretched beyond their capabilities and kept breaking down. We did what we could manually, but most days we couldn't confirm everything until we got back to the office. I found a trade that I couldn't match up. One of the girls had made a mistake on the trading floor. I had only just recruited her and I felt responsible for her. It wasn't necessarily her fault either. So I didn't make the phone call to London to tell them about the error because I felt responsible, and that's how the SIMEX 88888 account was born.

**IVAN**

What was this?

**NICK**

The SIMEX 88888 account was an account I had used to hide the bad position. We were left in the position that the markets were going to open up in the morning. If the markets opened up in our favour it would have made a small profit; if they opened up against us there would be a loss. So I was just hiding this account from the people in London and Tokyo, to see how the market opened up. The market opened up against us; there was a loss, and that was the beginning of the collapse of Barings. I thought that calling it the five eights account would be lucky! How wrong I was.

**IVAN**

So it was an illegal account?

**NICK**

Yes.

**IVAN**

Isn't it amazing how life can change so much from one

little act? Just one little decision goes wrong and years of your life are affected by it. Every day we face decisions like that. For example, deciding to talk to a stranger or not. If you *do* decide to talk to them you might end up marrying them and having children with them. Your whole life could be changed by that one decision. And it's the same with your decision to open that illegal account. Up to that point had you been basically honest in the commercial world, would you say? It wasn't your natural inclination to lie?

**NICK**

I don't think it was. Up to that stage I wasn't able to do such a thing anyway. I always took pride in my accuracy and diligence. My role was principally to look after the administrative side with an ever-increasing role in the trading operation. But in those early days it was supposed to be heavily weighted in the administrative and control functions. I knew that this was a twelve-hour thing. The market was going to open in the morning and I had, basically, a fifty–fifty shot at getting this girl out of trouble. I never expected the SIMEX 88888 account to last longer than a day because very simple checks were all that would be needed to expose it. And anybody could do those. It's the first thing you learn in the first day in the job, checking the positions, and anybody can walk into the office and do it at any time. The SIMEX 88888 account would be exposed because the positions I held for London wouldn't agree with those that I held at the exchange. It's a simple mathematical formula. Just ticking the things off. An eight-year-old could do it. And the fact that it wasn't done during a period of nearly three years is ultimately what led to the collapse of the bank. But, when it started, it really was a very short-term thing in my mind.

**IVAN**

How long from the opening of that account was it before the whole thing went belly-up?

**NICK**

Nearly three years.

**IVAN**

And throughout that time the position got worse?

**NICK**

Yes, well, during that period there was one occasion when I got it back to a profit. In May of 1993.

**IVAN**

And couldn't you, at that point, have cut your losses and closed the account?

**NICK**

Yeah, sure. In fact, I would have had a profit. So nobody would have minded; as long as the figures were black and not in the red nobody paid too much attention, just fantasised over how large their bonuses were going to be.

**IVAN**

And you wouldn't have ended up in prison?

**NICK**

No, I'd probably still be working for Barings. I don't have the answer to why I didn't close it. With hindsight I look back at most things that happened over those years and hopefully can re-rationalise them and see where I went wrong, hopefully learning from my mistakes. I know I wouldn't do it now. Probably the most important lesson for me has been to ask for help and advice when it's needed and not to muddle on.

**IVAN**

Well, perhaps you had got into a habit with it?

**NICK**

Definitely. And here we arrive back at my need for status again. This eclectic mix of Asian and ex-pat employees had bought into the whole success story, as much as I thought my wife of the time had. Exposing the lie would mean exposing me and the subsequent loss of status among my employees. The people that worked with me were my friends. I was an ex-pat, but I wasn't really part of the ex-pat financial scene. I had a few friends, mainly hoteliers, outside of the industry. But the Malayan and Chinese people who worked for me were the people I associated with in the evenings and at the weekends. So there was never really a proper manager–employee relationship. So when these people, my friends, made mistakes, every one went into the SIMEX 88888 account. I never reprimanded them; I never shouted at them. There was never any negative message sent to them for making an error.

**IVAN**

So you confused your social needs with the needs of management?

**NICK**

I presume so. But then, as I said, in May 1993, from something like a $25 million loss, I got it back. The 88888 account was into credit with a perfect expiry in the options; the markets closed at a most magnificent level for me with a quarter of a million pounds profit in the account, rather than a huge $25 million loss.

**IVAN**

And nobody would have been any the wiser about what had happened?

**NICK**

Not without interrogation of the accounts. I had to get rid of the quarter of a million pounds, but nobody in Tokyo was going to complain about that because, at the end of the day, it would go in their account and they were going to get paid a bonus out of it. This happened on a Friday, so I had the whole weekend to celebrate. But on the Monday people were making mistakes again.

**IVAN**

So you kept the illegal account going?

**NICK**

Yes, in the misguided belief that I could do it again. There were peaks and troughs, obviously, in the P&L (profit and loss) account from that day forward. And probably more peaks over the period. But there was, with hindsight, a blurring of social and business needs. There's a part in *Rogue Trader* where Ewan McGregor is looking in the mirror, splashing water on his face and repeating in a hysterical tone, 'I, Nicholas Leeson, lost £50 million in one day.' Apart from never calling myself Nicholas, after looking through the accounts with the liquidators, it appears that that was one of my better days! And there were many worse.

## IVAN

Confusing trying to be nice to people with the reality of running a business always cost *me* money. So I know it can happen. It's just that, in your case, the consequences were financially rather large.

## NICK

One of the reasons it happened on such a mega scale is that I had so much autonomy. The banks and other financial institutions are always looking for new ways to bend the rules, manipulate jurisdictions, to make more money. They are always pushing the frontiers. The Barings crash was an accident waiting to happen: the main reason it occurred, and why it will always be a major vulnerability for banks, is because the regulating and back-office control roles are far less glamorous. They don't have the status or the financial rewards, so normally have a less attractive pool of people to recruit from. They are a cost behind what's happening at the sharp end where money is made: where the brains and the power are. And that's a dangerous thing. The Barings collapse was just an extreme example of what can happen. Barings was exceptionally poorly run. They didn't have one adequate control, and most of the big financial institutions have hundreds. But the derivatives financial markets, with all the newly structured, constantly changing products and hybrids that they are trading in, had an inherent danger in them. No one really knew what was going on. To a degree, that continues to this day.

## IVAN

Such uncertainty must have contributed to raising everybody's stress levels. Too many possible outcomes to a decision, like having too much choice in the shops, create stress in people.

## NICK

Yes. I was always of the opinion that, post-Barings, such a crash should never, ever happen again. It should have been a wake-up call that nobody forgets. But unfortunately the pattern hasn't changed.

## IVAN

And since then we've had other huge scandals, like Enron.

## NICK

Sure. There are far too many to mention. I suppose I grew up thinking banks had an endless stream of money. By going to work in a bank when I left school, I thought I had a job for life. There's no such thing these days, but I grew up with that idea. I not only proved that is not the case but I also proved that banks aren't necessarily for life either.

## STATUS AND PECKING ORDERS

► Your status in a group reflects the amount of power you hold. Status distinctions usually emerge rapidly and they solidify over time in groups that last a long time, such as families and business organisations.

► Status distinctions emerge quickly in other primate groups as well, where power often reflects physical stature. In many species, status distinctions arise through physical confrontations or threats of confrontation, which result in a pecking order that each partner in a potential conflict recognises (or learns the hard way).

► We humans, like other animals, usually have little difficulty reading signs of status and recognising who defers to whom. People of high status tend to talk more and are freer to interrupt. They also display their status nonverbally, by standing erect, maintaining eye contact longer and generally displaying signs of confidence.

## STATUS AND TRIBAL GROUPS

There is no doubt that the longest part of the evolution of our minds and behaviour took place under circumstances when our ancestors were living in small, tribal groups – a situation that was essential for our survival. It should therefore be no surprise that tribalism is still a major factor in human thinking and behaviour.

Tribes have the following key characteristics:
- Individuals arise as authority figures exemplifying the values of the group
- These leaders have followers who accept those values as 'facts'
- The tribal group is glued together by attention exchange between the members
- Tribal members are the 'real people' – outsiders are considered to be less real (even sub-human).

You may think that the above is an incredibly primitive analysis of the organisation you work for, the country you live in or the ethnic group you were born to, and has nothing to do with sophisticated, modern people, with our complex high-tech organisations. However, evidence shows that the above factors are endemic in every human community and their influence is as powerful today as it has ever been.

## IVAN'S COMMENTARY

Our early ancestors quickly learned they would fall prey to any one of a wide range of powerful predators if they made themselves too vulnerable. Lions, leopards and packs of hyenas could easily have snuffed our species out, had we not evolved to coexist peacefully in large groups. Only a co-operative gang of humans – acting as a single organism – could make enough noise, throw enough rocks and wave enough burning sticks at predators to keep them at bay. So, back in primitive times, to be pushed out of the tribe meant you would not have the protection of the group – and this meant certain death.

The need to belong was so essential to our survival that it was programmed into us. This is why we still fear rejection, unless we are confident we have alternative groups to fall back on who will still accept us unconditionally. Today, the need to feel we belong and the need to have status in a group are two of the most basic human givens.

Without consciously being aware of it, we continually monitor our social position in all the various groups we belong to. Boys and girls seek peer-group approval in all stages of growing up. If they don't get it, anxiety and depression can set in; there are few things as sad as a child alone in a school playground without a friend in the world. And adults are no different. We all let it be known, in myriad ways, that we have friends and indicate what groups we belong to by the clothes we wear, the cars we drive, the way we speak, the lifestyle we lead and so on.

Within each group dominant figures arise: inspiring leaders who can take responsibility and hold the group together, bullies who use fear to maintain their position, trendsetters who amuse, innovators who help the group prosper, managers who try to make themselves indispensable to the group by organising its activities, and bureaucrats whose domination technique is to entangle everybody in complex rules and regulations.

To have high status has huge biological advantages. The higher your ranking, the healthier you are likely to be and the longer you will live. Research about the medical effects of status came from a study of many thousands of retired male civil servants. Their ranking in the Civil Service proved to be the best predictor of when they would die. The most high-ranking individuals survived into their eighties. The middle management died in their seventies. Those who made it only to clerical positions died off in their sixties. Even after factoring out the classic predictors of an early death (smoking, high blood pressure and being overweight), status was the most significant.

There is a clear, linear biological relationship between cholesterol levels, blood plaque levels and seniority of rank. People who are demoted and lose status, for example, have a five-fold rise in dangerous blood plaque levels that is known to be a factor in premature death and heart disease.

The most advanced individuals, of course, are *comfortable* slipping in and out of many different social groups, and *uncomfortable* with the primitive 'them and us' mindset that devalues people from other groups as 'outsiders'. They know how to be themselves in any group, from the privileged elite to the poorest of the poor. They adapt their behaviour according to circumstance, and do not mind giving up their status.

Since needs are the 'givens' of human nature, and therefore have to be fulfilled in the environment for people to mature in a fully rounded way, what happens when a need for status is *not* met? The answer is that greed can arise. Greed behaviour tends to appear in any individual or group when needs are not met in balance. If our need for attention is not met, for example, we become attention seekers, which can become destructive to relationships. We can become greedy for status if status has been denied us in childhood and adolescence, and this can develop into an aggressive drive to dominate others in order to extract status through power. Any healthy human *need*, if left unmet, can swell into a destructive *want*. In a mature society, the process of getting people's needs met would provide a natural rhythm of checks and balances to ensure no one becomes excessively greedy or cruel.

Greed is an emotion and, like all basic emotions, draws its strength from the fact that, in a fundamental way, it is directly linked to survival. Every living thing has to take from the environment around it to stay alive. This is why our greed can become overwhelmingly powerful. Like all emotional states, when we become greedy for status, our attention is focused and locked and we are unable to see the bigger picture – what's really happening – and do what's necessary.

In my opinion, the main reason Barings Bank collapsed is the psychological naivety of those responsible for putting Nick Leeson into the position they did. The Singapore operation was a small tribe within a larger tribe, and therefore another opportunity for leaders with status to emerge. When immature people have status, earned or not, they will not be inclined to let it go and will do anything, *anything*, to keep it, because their psychological and physical health depends upon it. Nick Leeson was the most perfect example of someone desperately trying to hang on to a position. He was not trying to destroy a bank; he was trying to maintain his status.

# chapter 4
# ISOLATION AND CONFINEMENT – hard times in a Singapore jail

## NICK'S STORY

Coming to terms with incarceration was initially the most difficult thing I'd ever had to cope with in my life. Leaving school and starting work in my chosen career had offered endless possibilities and never in my wildest dreams had I imagined having a brush with the law. I'd often think of all the positive things I could do with my life but I'd never entertained the idea that events would turn out so catastrophically negative. My mother dying when I was twenty had been the hardest thing I'd had to cope with prior to the Barings fiasco, but at the time of her death I was already propelling myself career-wise towards some of the targets she had set me. Thankfully she never saw how far I deviated from that path and how disastrously I fell from grace, eventually becoming incarcerated in first a German, then a Singaporean jail.

Secreted in my cell in Frankfurt at the far end of Block A, I felt as though I had lost everything. I was positioned at the extreme outer perimeter of the prison; I could even see people going about their daily business in the taller houses that bordered the prison yard, but it would have been impossible to feel any more isolated. I spent day upon day crying, and at times it felt as if the tears would never stop. The brazen young lad depicted in the movie *Rogue Trader*, passing hand signals to the waiting throng at Frankfurt Airport just before he is taken into custody, is an absolute myth. The tough exterior was gone and the slightest thing would trigger a stream of tears until I was all cried out. There was no pride left; I was on my own and wave after wave of emotion flooded through me. I cried for me; I cried for Lisa; I cried for the mother I had lost; there were times when I cried purely because there was nothing else to do.

The cell door was locked behind me, and somebody else chose when it would open. They would choose when I ate; they decided when I could sleep; they even regulated when I could have a shower and when I went to the toilet. All of the personal choices that one has in life were taken away from me. I felt lonely; I felt lost and deserted but, worst of all, I knew I had virtually no control over what was going to happen to me. And that realisation was the most damning and damaging to me as a person.

Being locked up in Germany had been hard, but at least a prisoner was accorded basic human rights. If I needed something, I could apply to the courts to decide on the necessity. The prison in Singapore would afford me no such luxury; the law there was applied to everyone in the same manner. Nine months into my remand in Germany, the realisation that I was going to have to return to the place I had tried so hard to escape was beginning to cast an ever-darkening shadow over my fate. That shadow was long and perversely comforting at first, as I convinced myself we could postpone or even avoid the inevitable. It protected me. But day by day the shadow was shortening and the reality of my return was beginning to scare me to death.

The thought of suicide was a constant companion during my time in Hoechst, alternating between being the last possible solution and, at times of the deepest despair, the only option open to me. I even thought about the logistics of it. I knew where it was going to happen – the showers on our block – although not exactly when; that would have been far too much information for me to cope with. Rationally, one would avoid the place where one's life was going to end, but I wasn't going to avoid the showers for the rest of my incarceration. Someone else could decide the when. I had only to arrange the payment, which seemed a paltry sum. It wasn't the easiest thing to bring into a conversation, but I was quite friendly with two Italian prisoners on my block – junior Mafiosi who plied their trade in the underworld of Frankfurt. They would handle the arrangements; I just had to sort out the payment. That was really how desperate I had become. I'd already coped with the shame of Barings collapse, better than I would have imagined possible, but the thought of returning to an extremely long sentence in Singapore was a step too far.

Speaking to Lisa and my father about it during a visit had felt like an out-of-body experience; I could hear my voice, feel my lips moving, but couldn't really believe what I was saying. The newspapers were speculating on the length of sentence I would receive. It was frightening. Numbers flew out of the pages of every newspaper I picked up: fourteen, twenty-one, eighty-four years – there was no consistency to the speculation but, although they couldn't agree on a tariff, I knew for sure that I would be in jail for a long time.

I just didn't want it to be in Singapore. Although it no doubt ranked among the top-ten upmarket tourist destinations in the world, very few tourists experienced the murky underworld I was about to enter. The few simple privileges I had in Germany would become mere memories. I wouldn't be able to hang the milk outside the window to keep it cool any more; the stifling heat in Singapore would turn it – if not me – sour during my incarceration. The laptop, the GameBoy, the television, radio and newspapers that I treasured would all be lost. Censorship was the order of the day in the Singaporean prison: a 56-page newspaper was often reduced to nothing more than a couple of pages.

As bad as Germany had been in those first few weeks, in returning to Singapore to be sentenced I was stepping into the unknown again, and that was something I found difficult to cope with. Time had quickened up over those last few weeks and the life I had reluctantly become used to was slipping away. I liked things in black and white; I wanted to know what was going to happen tomorrow, the next day and every day thereafter. The devil I knew was something I could face; the devil I didn't scared me to death. This was the sickest I had ever felt – a dull pain in my stomach and sour taste in my mouth were ever present. It was the most scared I had ever been. I was knowingly returning to a regime whose reputation I had severely tarnished, and they would want to inflict the severest punishment.

We'd hatched a deal with the Singaporean authorities in terms of the sentence I would receive, but believing they would keep to it was a massive leap of faith. The charges were going to be reduced from twelve to two and I was told I would face a maximum of eight years in prison. With the standard remission of a third, that equated to five years and four months. That was a number I could get my head around. I was told they wouldn't have been able to do anything worse. Assurances and reassurances from my legal team fell on deaf ears, though; I couldn't take anything as a definite. I hadn't slept properly in weeks. The stress of that last month had been unbearable. I looked as haggard as the prison-issue clothes that hung on my body: washed, rewashed and passed from inmate to inmate.

I exercised more and more as the date of my return approached. I wanted to be fit and healthy, mentally ready to face the challenges that lay ahead. There isn't too much exercise that you can do in a small cell but I'd invent them. Another inmate was allowed an old-fashioned typewriter. It was heavy, and I'd borrow it and use it as a weight to exercise my arms. I didn't know what physical or mental threats my return to Singapore held, but I wanted to be ready for them. I read late into the night in the hope that sleep would come. But more often than not it didn't.

Leaving Hoechst Prison on that last frosty November morning in 1995 my Singaporean lawyer regaled me with stories of what incarceration would be like. There would be karaoke, he said, with worthwhile recreation and time being easy to pass. But I was not so easily taken in by his positive spin on what awaited me. Dingy prison cells that we had nicknamed 'Little Beirut' during my time in Hoechst were the best I was expecting.

Everything that happened afterwards is a blur – the journey to the airport in Frankfurt merging into the thirteen-hour plane journey back to Singapore. None of it felt real. I was carried along in the whirlwind of activity that was happening around me. I was sitting in Business Class of a Singaporean aeroplane, drinking champagne and eating a specially prepared meal. None of it made sense. I could smell the food but it had no taste. I could feel the bubbles of the champagne trickle down my throat but I was numb to everything that was happening around me. I actually hungered for the reality of the situation that awaited me so I could start coming to terms with it. There was no point hiding from the situation; it needed to be dealt with, and I needed to start doing just that. Sure, it scared me to death, but putting my head in the sand wasn't going to make it go away.

As the onboard entertainment system slowly counted down the kilometres left until our arrival in Singapore, I became more and more dogged about what awaited me. I was going to hold my head up high and take what was coming on the chin, determined I was going to see this through. Stepping on that plane had cemented that course and I wasn't going to quit.

During the last six months of my manic trading in Singapore I'd always known I would end up in jail if I didn't manage to get myself out of trouble. My lawyer mentioned on a number of occasions that I was his easiest client because I never professed my innocence – I only ever wanted to know how long I was going to have to serve so I could come to terms with it. Now, after nine months of not knowing, the sentencing in the Singaporean court meant I knew that, with the standard remission, I was facing five years and four months in prison. It was going to be incredibly tough but, after some heavy soul-searching, I steeled myself to face it. As much as my lawyers talked about lower sentences, I was ready for the worst outcome. Stephen Pollard, my British lawyer, had been the voice of sanity and reason throughout this terrible time, and he remained the most realistic, believing I could get a minimum of six years. My Singaporean lawyer suggested I may get as little as eighteen months, but my first night in a Singaporean cell without a karaoke machine indicated how wrong he was. As we passed through a specially arranged customs area in Changi Airport, there were no questions about how long I wanted to stay, but a knowing nod of the head gave the silent message: 'We'll let you know.'

I just prayed that it wasn't going to be too long, and I forced a weak smile back. If anything had been more misleading than the positions I had carried at Barings, then it was that smile.

A day later some documents were signed and I was handed over to the court police. As my minders for the last thirty hours made to depart, I was ushered through a door into a vacant room. The door clanged shut with a finality I was becoming used to. The cells were dark and dingy and, rather than being purposely built, they looked as though they had been carved out of a mound of stone. The cells in Germany were said to have been over a hundred years old and had been used in both world wars. But, as old as they were, they had at least been light and airy. My mind fast-forwarded to spending the next five years in a dungeon such as this and the strong exterior I'd cultivated to face my sentence evaporated. I felt the dark forces of depression welling up to occupy a position at the front of my thoughts. My body was trembling and I was sweating profusely. My eyes were wet with tears but I knew that, if I started to cry, I might never stop. I felt as if I was going to explode and wave upon wave of fear rushed over me, pulling me deeper and deeper into despair. Perhaps I wouldn't be able to cope after all, and this was my worst possible nightmare – the complete loss of control. I hadn't thought it was going to be this bad, but it was promising to be worse than anything I'd dared imagine back in Germany, and there was nothing I could do to stop the rollercoaster of my fate. It was following a path I had no influence over. I wanted to get off the ride but, of course, that was impossible.

The cell seemed to be getting smaller; the walls were closing in and I was seeing shadows and shapes out of the corner of my eye. My mind was playing tricks on me. Prisoners were shouting in other cells and their voices were ringing through my head, adding to the pressure. I'd always been slightly claustrophobic but had never experienced anything as disorientating as this. I wanted to scream. I couldn't cope. I wanted to hit the walls, with my hands, my head. I needed to do something but my options were non-existent. When things had got on top of me in Germany I had exercised. I'd run on the spot for hours, carefully counting each pair of steps that I made, sometimes imagining there was a football on the floor, and actually stepping from one side to another around the 'ball'. Press-ups had been another coping mechanism, but neither of those was viable here. To add to the incongruity, for the first time in nine months I had a shirt and tie on. I looked as though I was ready for a day on the trading floor rather than a day in front of the judge.

My heart was racing and I needed to bring it to a level that was more manageable. Gingerly I placed both arms on the slab of a seat and gained purchase to propel myself to my feet. My arms quivered with a combination of the exertion and the fear that was coursing through my veins but I managed to get to my feet. I started to walk the length of the cell, towards the gated bars of the door and back to the wall that marked the limits of my domain. Four steps were all that was possible. Back and forth I paced, concentrating on how many times I could walk from end to end to take my mind off everything else that was worrying me. The gate and back was one circuit. I counted until I got bored; I didn't have the patience I'd had in Frankfurt. Six or seven hundred laps of the cell was all I could muster and then I flopped back on to the slab of stone that was the only resting point on offer. There was no clock to be seen and, not knowing the patterns of the holding cells, there was no way I could even guess the time.

There was no point looking for a nail to bite – they'd starting going when the first couple of thousand dollars had exited the accounts at Barings, and I'd never been in a good position for long enough for them to grow back. The tattered remains of skin around my fingernails were a representation of the tatters my life was in. The dark, damp odour of the holding cell contrasted sharply with the brilliant sunshine and freshness that lay little more than twenty metres away, but the fact that I couldn't move from one to the other shot home the realisation that I no longer had any control over what was happening to me.

Richard Magnus, the judge, delivered my sentence with all the pomposity the event afforded. I never paid too much attention to him; my eyes were closed and I was on tenterhooks waiting for the number that would precede the word 'years' to rationalise what awaited me. Six and a half years was the sentence, four years and four months for good behaviour and I'd already served nine months in Germany. Finally I had a target. I knew what I had to do. Leaving the court after my sentence I was quickly handcuffed by the waiting guards and led away to be transferred to Tanah Merah Maximum Security Prison. The indignity of the handcuffs was quickly surpassed by having to be strip-searched and squat five times over an upturned mirror so that they could check my anal passage for contraband. I've no idea what they thought I may have been carrying but I reckoned I must have missed my vocation if I had managed to smuggle something halfway across the world, under the noses of four separate police forces, through two different prisons and two separate police stations.

The isolation I felt in prison was overwhelming. I remember being sent to my room as a child and being totally unable to cope with the penalty – the boredom of doing nothing and not knowing quite how long I was going to be there. That punishment lasted hours at the most, but this was going to be considerably longer. I'd never been well enough equipped to pass those hours alone in the bedroom. I certainly didn't think I had the tools at my disposal to cope with many thousands of times those periods. I'd started a long, arduous journey uphill and was well aware that there was still a long way to go to reach the summit. My mother's death had probably been the loneliest period of my life, but at least then friends had rallied around and got me through the darkest days. But now, like never before, I was going to be totally alone, far from family, friends or even a familiar culture. The prison housed something like fifteen hundred inmates, and there was only one Briton – me.

## IN CONVERSATION

**IVAN**

Being imprisoned in Germany must have got you accustomed to prison life.

**NICK**

Germany wasn't as hard as Singapore, so it broke me into that life. But what did hit me in Germany was the loss of freedom. They closed the doors and I realised I had no control. That was the massive thing that hit me like a bolt. For the first six months I cried a lot, experiencing intense frustration. I was feeling sorry for myself, not knowing what was going on outside, with Lisa, with my family. I felt remorse and sorrow for what I'd done to the bank and everything that happened. That sorrow was uncontrollable. On Sundays I'd blub all day, but I must have got all that emotion out of my system because I haven't cried since I left Germany. Sundays were bad days. We weren't allowed out of our rooms on Sundays, except to go to a church service.

**IVAN**

One newspaper article said you'd found God in prison.

**NICK**

I'm not religious, never have been, and don't think I ever will be. In fact, the way they preach religion in prison pushed me further away from it. I do think there is some higher being, though I've no idea what it is or where it is or how it works. I went to the services on a couple of occasions as a way of coping, because otherwise we were not allowed out of our cells at all on Sundays. Anybody who's been in a fairly desperate situation will see why I did that. The rest of the week we were allowed out; we did a bit of work, had exercise and sport sessions and we had a TV hour. But on Sundays, nothing. So I went to services, but not through any desire to find God. The media invented all that. There was also a lot of religious teaching when I was in the Singaporean prison. But I was sceptical of that activity because the prisoners they were preaching to were at their lowest ebb. If they wanted to convert people to Christianity or Islam or whatever, the challenge should be to do it when they're in the real world; when they're feeling good about themselves and searching for something. In Germany I was in a cell on my own. I think that all-pervading sense of loneliness really dragged me down but I never turned to religion.

**IVAN**

So you didn't have any support from other prisoners?

**NICK**

No. In the cell in Singapore there was me and two others, both Chinese. The cell was six feet by fifteen feet with a small latrine area. There was enough room for the three of us to lie down, but nothing else. Everyone in the prison was a gang member, apart from me. Crying just wasn't done. It would be a massive loss of face, the concept that Asian society survives on. Everybody had to maintain face. Losing face would mean weakness, and nowhere in the world is weakness taken advantage of more than in prison. Prior to speaking to you I would have said that it was my own pride that made sure I didn't let myself down in front of these people. But I can see now that there is a biological *need* for status, even within that small cell with just two other prisoners. I needed status and crying was not the way to get it. Had I done so, everyone in the prison would have known within an hour. So I never cried in Singapore, not even when I was diagnosed with cancer.

**IVAN**

So how did you get your need for status met in Singapore?

**NICK**

I suppose I had status before I arrived because of what I had done and the huge amount of money involved – more money than even the biggest gang leader had been involved with. I never fed on it or propagated the myth but equally I never denied any of the rumours that were flying around. In itself, that gave some credence to the stories and catapulted my own prison status to the stratosphere.

**IVAN**

They must have been in awe of you.

**NICK**

They were a bit. The newspapers had created myths about how I had secreted millions of pounds in bank accounts around the world – accounts that I knew didn't exist. So I had a kind of status. The throne was there; I just had to sit on it.

## IVAN

Under the circumstances, any normal person would do the same to survive.

## NICK

Prison is about survival. You have to search high and low for things you can use to your advantage. And that's what I did. Because of my story the guards wanted to speak to me. Not only the guards. The officers themselves had me on half-hour watch for the first two or three months. Everyone in the prison knew I was being watched over. I never got any preferential treatment. I didn't want any, either, but the high level of surveillance gave me another form of status. The only preferential treatment I got was when I was diagnosed with colon cancer, and that was because I fought for it.

## IVAN

The more needs that are met in any given situation, the better the chances of staying sane and surviving.

## NICK

I must be the living embodiment of that. I never knew that my needs were being met at the time but, with hindsight, I can see how I managed to contrive the best from a very dismal situation and get those needs met in any way I could. The worst thing for me in the German prison was that I used to get ten newspapers or so a day because my lawyer would send them in to me – on remand I had more rights than I would after sentencing. There were long stories about what they were discovering at Barings. And a lot of them would be false. I used to speed-read them and didn't really want to know too much about what was going on. But during that whole period we never negoti- ated with the Singaporeans, so I didn't know how long I was going to be in prison, and that was the worst thing. For a while I had hoped I'd get back to England. But there were so many unanswered questions. All it was, every day, was questions, questions, questions. And there were no definite answers. I can cope with things that are definite. I hate it when things are wishy-washy. I need a concrete starting point. Without one I didn't have a chance. I knew I was going to jail. My lawyer said, 'You're the first client I've ever had who knew he was going to jail. Everybody else thinks they are innocent.'

**IVAN**

You knew you had to pay the price for what you did?

**NICK**

I knew that. But what drove me up the wall was the ques- tion of where was I going to jail and for how long. The newspapers were speculating that I would get 84 years, but nobody really knew. I tried to get my head round what that could mean. I was 28 when I was arrested in Germany. Fourteen years in prison would make me 42 when I got out. Eighty-four years would make me dead. It was at this point that the thoughts of suicide arose.

**IVAN**

In Germany? Before you went to Singapore?

**NICK**

Yes, principally in Germany. Once I'd been sent to Singapore and sentenced, I knew where I was and I could cope with it. I had a starting point.

**IVAN**

I think you're so right. People cannot think or act unless they have something concrete to work on.

**NICK**

You write about something similar in your book, when you describe how politicians talk in an abstract way, using what you call nominalisations – saying things that sound as if they're meaningful, but there's nothing solid about them.

**IVAN**

That's right. They use abstract nouns – words with no substance that make people feel good, or certain, about what is being said. For example, 'truth', 'freedom', 'aspiration', 'love', 'terrorism', 'change', 'innovations', 'principles', 'equality' etc. – the type of word that muddles clear communication by appearing to be something concrete when it is not. They create a feeling in listeners that something meaningful is being said when it isn't. The problem when you hear a word like this is that, because it contains no concrete information, you have to go on an inner search and pattern-match to what it means to you personally, based on your own past experience. Inevitably, such a word will mean different things to different people – one person's 'aspiration', for example, is not the same as another's. Once pattern matched we put our own meaning on it, which is automatically 'tagged' with an emotion. Our emotions are stirred but not connected up to anything tangible. We assume the politician is talking about *our* perception, but he's not. It's a trick. However, it is largely an unconscious process but you found out about the necessity for concrete thinking in a very personal way.

**NICK**

I had to experience it first. I kept saying to my lawyer, 'We have to negotiate with the Singaporeans, we *have* to.' He'd say, 'No. Let's exhaust this avenue first. We're using such and such as a bargaining tool. We'll say we're going back to England; *they* are going to have to come to us and do the deal.' But I was unhappy with the unease that gave me. I had an absolutely massive sense of release when we finally did the negotiation with the Singaporeans, after six months of not knowing. They came down to a maximum of eight years, which meant I'd spend five years and four months in prison. I was OK with that. I thought I could do it. I knew it would be tough. But I was basing my expectations of prison on what the environment was like in Germany. Big mistake!

**IVAN**

You had a proper bed in the German prison?

**NICK**

A bed. A radio. A TV. A laptop. That's how I wrote *Rogue Trader* – on the laptop they provided. So my expectation was unfounded but, in terms of the period of time I thought I could cope with, everything was very clear to me. Of course, most lawyers give you a totally unrealistic perception of what is going to happen to you, and of your chances of succeeding. I think most lawyers have a massive tendency to tell you what you want to hear. I don't want to hear what I *want* to hear: I want to be told the truth. I want to know what's really going to happen.

**IVAN**

How did confinement affect your mental state?

**NICK**

Well, as I've said, there were times in prison when I
wanted to end it all.

**IVAN**

That bad?

**NICK**

Yes. The first week I was on remand in Frankfurt I was
locked up 23 hours a day for observation. Which was normal, although I didn't know that at the time. I had one
book for company. Nobody came round to give me books
to pass the time. I had a Tom Clancy thriller on me when
I was arrested. Food was delivered to the cell, three meals
a day, and there were no visitors. It was a sterile environment: the walls were clean and painted clinical colours –
pale yellows and greens and whites. A radio was attached
to the wall and had one German channel on all the time. I
got to know a few of the songs but there was a lot that
passed me by. So I read and reread the Tom Clancy book,
once a day, during the course of that week.

**IVAN**

And you can't remember it?

**NICK**

No, which is strange because normally, when I read a
book, I can pretty much tell you everything about it.
But during that period I was so emotional and confused
by what was happening and the maelstrom of events

bombarding me all the time that I would sit there doggedly reading away and, after twenty minutes, I'd think, What happened in the last ten pages? My eyes were scanning the printed words but they weren't centre stage. The book was a tool I used to fill the time. I had massive emotional lows during that time. The only thing that broke them up for me was my lawyer visiting. This is something that's stayed with me throughout the various cells and prisons I've been in. I would get distressed and depressed. Distressed sums it up rather well; I was totally flustered. I just needed to step back and be doing something, otherwise I'd be swamped with depressing thoughts that I couldn't shake off and I'd spin into a negative spiral. I'm no intellectual but I'm rational enough to see when something is harming me. My negative thoughts were obviously causing me a lot of discomfort and distress. I wanted to hit the wall. I wanted to hit the cupboard. I wanted to pull something down and smash it. It's a destructive feeling that on a lot of occasions can be turned into self-destruction. I'm sure that's why some people self-harm. I certainly saw that within the prison: people taking razor blades to themselves and trying to cut their wrists and suchlike. I was a bit callous about that in the German prison. There were 'attempted' suicides – but very much *attempted*. Those people weren't making concerted efforts to do the job properly! They just gave themselves superficial cuts and scratches. When things were getting on top of me I knew I mustn't harm myself. I wasn't going to slash my wrists. I wasn't going to bash my head against the walls, because it would hurt me more than the wall. But I had to do *something*. So I used to spend hours walking up and down and counting each step like a mantra.

**IVAN**

You went into a trance?

**NICK**

Yes. It got to that, although not in the initial observation period. Later, when I was in a cell on my own, exercise was the way. I had more room and improvised ways to exercise. On certain days I was allowed a shower. I had a bin in there and I'd jump over it. I'd run on the spot and walk up and down. I discovered that walking up and down the cell seven hundred times took an hour. And I could pass an hour that way by setting myself positive targets and achieving them. As mind-numbingly boring as it must sound to people who've never experienced it, it helped me through those difficult times when negative feelings welled up and I felt hot and panicky. That's when I needed to divert my thoughts and focus on something. In solitary confinement I just walked up and down endlessly. I could hear different bells ringing in various parts of the prison: a bell for breakfast time, a bell for lunchtime and one for the mid-morning muster when they'd check the numbers of inmates to make sure no one had escaped. These bells went off like clockwork, so I knew exactly what the time was and could start my walking again and keep myself occupied.

**IVAN**

That strategy would have satisfied your need to feel you had some control over events. Psychologists have researched survivors of terrible torture regimes in South American prisons. They found that those who survived well mentally were the ones who devised ways of feeling they had some element of control over what was happening, even during the actual torture. For example, they would count to five internally before they screamed. The torturer couldn't stop that because he didn't know the prisoner was doing it. But, according to the psychologists, that slender thread of control kept the prisoners from going insane. Those who didn't devise such strategies were mentally scarred for life when they got out. Fortunately nowadays we can de-traumatise victims of torture and post-traumatic stress disorder but they didn't know how to do that back in the seventies when the research was done.

## NICK

There were people in the Singapore prison with sentences that just aren't handed out in England. One guy had a 38-year sentence and he was resigned to it. Others had life sentences, and life meant life – no chance of release. So they knew they would die in prison. It was said that after three and a half to four years prisoners cross the border-line, crack and become institutionalised. I spent longer inside than that and I didn't. One of the great advantages for me was that the mass of letters I received ensured that I never felt too removed from society or too isolated. But I did see people having great difficulty if their sentences were longer than the four-year period. Obviously control over even the basics, like washing and eating, is taken away from you when you are confined in a prison. And there's not much you can do to change that. But controlling my exercise routine was one of the most powerful psychological tools that got me through. So having some control, as you say, meets a vital human need. A huge frustration for me in the Singaporean prison was that all prisoners were allowed to have a shower between the hours of seven and eight in the morning. The prison was designed for between six and eight hundred people and so was the water supply. The prison, however, held fifteen hundred of us. But they still turned the water on at seven and turned it off at eight. The water tanks would empty and some halls would get no water. But that didn't stop a junior guard coming round at eight o'clock and turning off the water supply. He had his rules to follow and it was more than his job was worth to do anything else. And that's the way the whole city of Singapore is run too. Rules are followed blindly and you're not allowed to interpret them according to circumstances. It frustrated the life out of me and I'd drive myself mad ranting and railing against it but it never got me anywhere. I had to get to a stage where it didn't bother me too much if the water didn't arrive. I didn't experience such frustration in the German prison. Perhaps the western approach allows people to interpret rules more reasonably. But that kind of thinking aroused huge anger in me. I wanted revenge! I wanted to confront that person with his stupidity when he turned the tap off. That was my natural reaction.

**IVAN**

And it *is* completely natural. It doesn't mean you're an angry person generally.

## NICK

No. I'm not. One doesn't have to be a type-A personality to get angry. Just about every westerner would have the same response to such irrational blinkered rule-following. I went crazy at first but it quickly became apparent that was self-defeating because it only made me feel worse. Expressing anger didn't change anything under such circumstances. And so I had to keep myself under control. It's a key word, 'control'. And I had to control the way I was feeling. It's probably from that small seed at the beginning of my confinement in Singapore that my philosophy of life started to develop into the way I am now. I recognised that there were some things I couldn't do anything about.

## IVAN

It's the same lesson King Canute taught at the seaside when he demonstrated to his sycophantic followers that he couldn't stop the tide coming in.

## NICK

Exactly right. You have to be realistic. I had to willingly give up control over things I couldn't influence and seek control in those areas of my prison life that I *could* do something about: structuring my exercise, reading and diary- and letter-writing. By setting myself little targets and achieving them I stretched myself physically and mentally.

## STRESS REDUCER

**Accept what you can't change**
Keep in mind at all times the perennial truth that some situations, and some people, you can do nothing about. The reason this is important is that, when you want things to be different, you set up expectations charged with emotion in your autonomic nervous system and then, when what you want to happen does not happen as you expect it should, you will experience frustration and tenseness – stress. Have the courage to accept an imperfect world. Realise that life isn't always fair. Circumstances always alter cases. Be flexible, 'roll with the punches' with a positive attitude, despite hardships.

**IVAN**

The heat must have made it harder.

**NICK**

It did. And the rules meant you couldn't even make a paper fan to cool yourself with. That was mind-blowing to me. Did you know that you can make glue from rice? It would never have occurred to me, but you just mix water and rice and it becomes sticky. Then you can glue pages of magazines together so they become like thin card and fold them into fans. The Chinese and Malay prisoners all knew how to do this so they could keep themselves cool. Some of them got even more creative and did origami to pass the time. It didn't harm anybody. But we were only allowed things in our cells that the authorities had authorised. Whenever they checked the cells and found these harmless fans they'd rip them up.

## IVAN

But however bad it got you didn't think of it as depression at the time?

## NICK

It was only when I got out and read about depression that I realised I *had* been seriously depressed at certain times in prison. I'd wake up feeling down, knowing that I had over a thousand days more like that to go and really not want to go on any more. There'd be hundreds of emotions coursing through my body, trying to overpower me, but I managed to keep them at bay. There were days like birthdays, Christmas, anniversaries, where I had to submit but I did that knowing that I'd come back fighting the next day. I very quickly became conscious of the fact that, once you start a negative spiral of thinking, allowing yourself to feel bad, it's difficult to stop. I went several times to the point of suicidal despair, but I was lucky: I pulled myself back from the brink.

## IVAN

That's exactly what people have to do to stop chronic depression taking hold. The fact that you could do that, even in those dire circumstances, confirms depression is a self-generated phenomenon. Feeling low is common and natural. I doubt if anyone on this planet hasn't had a few days when they've felt things aren't going well.

**NICK**

I think it's OK to be depressed for a short time. People say to me, 'Don't you wake up every morning feeling worried and depressed?' but I don't. I am remorseful about every-thing that happened – more than anybody in the world – not least because it completely messed up my life at the time. But not depressed as such. Not clinically. I prefer my life now, even though I'm not worry-free. I was never more worried than during the birth of my baby. That was frightening. When I stood in front of the judge and was sentenced to six and a half years in prison, I'd got my mind around it beforehand, so there wasn't too much he could do to hurt me. But I really wasn't prepared for the birth of my child and what it entailed. *That* was scary.

**IVAN**

People are termed *clinically* depressed when they have a very low mood and take no pleasure in their usual inter-ests for a period of two weeks or more. This is also cou-pled with other symptoms such as sleep disturbance, loss of energy and motivation, feelings of worthlessness or guilt, difficulties in thinking and recurrent thoughts of death or suicide. Obviously you had many low-mood days in prison, but would you say you went into a period of chronic depression?

**NICK**

No, I don't believe I was ever clinically depressed. I was always conscious of how I felt and of how quickly my situation could make me feel depressed. But something always happened to bring me back from the brink of serious depression. A letter would arrive, for example, and I'd feel a certain kind of closeness to people again, that I hadn't been totally deserted and that there were things to look forward to. That would bring me back. And so did exercise. I could be feeling bad at eight o'clock in the morning with the pressure of everything so great that I wanted to implode and disappear. I could just about cope with how enclosed and small my cell was but there were certain mornings when the heat beating through the bars would be overly oppressive and compound the already cramped feeling. The lack of room and the heat would be boiling my brain and it would be near impossible to keep a lid on it. If I exploded, I knew I'd lash out: mindless violence is something I totally disagree with, so I'd sit quietly in a corner, looking inwards for peace and calm rather than outwards at anything that may annoy me. I'd wait agonisingly for the guard to open the door and release the tension. As soon as I exercised, the release of endorphins would bring me back to my senses.

## IVAN

It might surprise people that you didn't get seriously depressed.

## NICK

I didn't. Not for long periods like you're talking about. I don't know many people who have suffered from clinical depression, so it's difficult for me to draw a direct comparison but I suspect that a lot of the situations I found myself in would have overwhelmed many people. There were times when what I was undergoing – the loss of freedom as well as divorce, cancer and the collapse of the bank – totally crushed and overwhelmed me and I struggled to see a single piece of good news. I probably felt a lot, lot lower at those times than most depressed people, but for a shorter period of time. Something would happen that meant I was always able to bring myself back from becoming chronically depressed. In the punishment cells I'd sing. I must be the worst singer that I know – I barely know the words to half a song, but I'd cobble them together in some form or another and sing both to pass the time and divert my thoughts. 'Sitting on the Dock of the Bay' became a favourite, not because I liked it but because I found the words in a book and memorised them. At other times I'd draw. Now, art and me are strange bedfellows: my artistic skills are probably on a par with a six- or seven-year-old child's. Looking back, drawing was probably the most uncharacteristic thing I did – but it occupied me and stopped me from dwelling on the negatives.

**IVAN**

You'd find something else to think about?

**NICK**

That's it. I was always able to put my foot on the brake. As I progressed through my sentence, the time I had left to serve was always my biggest hurdle. Four and a half years was quickly transferred into months and, by the time I arrived in Singapore, it wasn't long before I could start to think in terms of breaking a thousand days. That was a milestone for me. Setting and achieving targets helped.

Removing a digit from the number of days I had left to go made it less scary; more achievable. Chunks of fifty days were a big thing, getting from a thousand to nine hundred and fifty days. Compartmentalising the time gave me a feeling of control so the length of sentence didn't have such an overpowering influence on my mood.

Being diagnosed with cancer, when I had nobody around to support me, was the biggest challenge to rational thinking. I was told the person in the bed to my left had AIDS; the person to my right had a bad case of tuberculosis. There wasn't a great deal that was positive, that I could take out of where I was and the situation I was in. The small degrees of control I'd gathered around me in my prison cell all disappeared once I was in the hospital ward.

**IVAN**

*And* you were shackled to the bed!

**NICK**

Yes. So I couldn't exercise. I even had to put my hand up to have a wee. Because of the operation I was back to infancy stage in terms of the support I needed, but surrounded by guards who didn't give a shit about me. When I was recovering from the operation I was on a pretty heavy dose of morphine and I would wander in and out of consciousness. After about four days they stopped the morphine but I still hankered for it. I suppose it must have been like going 'cold turkey'. For security reasons – so that I couldn't pass a message on to a well-meaning nurse or doctor – I had a prison officer posted by the side of my bed. As the lack of morphine took effect, I started to feel nauseous. I asked for the sick bag but unfortunately not quickly enough. A green slime projected its way at force on to the officer's tunic. No emotional needs of mine were being met in the hospital. The nurses were scared to talk to me because, if they did, they'd get barked at by some of the guards. They'd administer the medicine and bring the food and that was pretty much it. I made my own amusement. Some of the guards were half my size: under five feet tall and not at all well built. But they had guns and that gave them superiority. I just used to laugh inwardly and draw humour out of the way they behaved. Being escorted to the hospital for my chemotherapy was the funniest thing; you would have thought I had Arnold Schwarzenegger and Dolph Lundgren by my side instead of these two little guys. I could probably have picked one up in each arm and carried them along.

**IVAN**

It seems to me that, despite your awful situation, you discovered for yourself many of the techniques which are used to get people out of depression fast: stop the worrying, exercise, humour, getting some degree of control over events, being as rational as possible. Depression is not a disease. When people get on with life, and match up their innate needs in the world as best they can, they don't get depressed. You instinctively knew that you could survive if you set targets. Every day brought you nearer to freedom. You saw that life could be good again.

## NICK

I survived the collapse of the bank, prison, divorce, cancer, vilification and suggestions that I'm a psychopath, and pretty much everything else that's been thrown at me ever since – all huge stressors – and am the living embodiment of the fact that what doesn't kill you can only make you stronger. I do totally believe that. I have the inner strength to face pretty much anything. Everybody has the possibility of acquiring that strength if they survive difficult experiences that give them a bigger perspective.

## IVAN

I can't help noticing we're not talking any more about how you haven't changed!

## NICK

All I've talked about is how I *have* changed. I totally see that as we're talking. One of the things that hasn't changed is that I'd still help my friends. If someone needed my help, I'd go out of my way to give it and may take a few chances for them. But I've drawn a very clear line now where that risk becomes personal. I'd never overstep that, as the impact on my family would be unimaginable. Throughout the collapse of the bank I was ensconced in a small cell and it wasn't until I was released that I realised quite how much impact my actions had had on those people around me.

## IVAN

The difficulty with that as a way of thinking is that it's very difficult to really know what is help and what isn't. Smacking a child for running out on to a busy road, for example, can be seen as cruel, and the child certainly doesn't think you're helping him. But if it stops him from running into the path of a car it's being cruel to be kind. You'd be being nasty because you love him.

## NICK

I have difficulty with that conundrum: not knowing whether I'm helping someone or not. I had a persistently recurring dream when I was in prison. In the dream the bank hadn't collapsed; there were losses; somebody had come to the offices in Singapore and exposed the 88888 account. There was a big hullabaloo within the bank and I was called back to London to see the management. They had all the documentation there and they were going on about the £862-million loss. They reprimanded me but then said, 'It's OK. We're going to send you back to Singapore and you can carry on.' Actually, to anybody who's watched the film *Rogue Trader*, which accurately depicts how bad the management of the bank was, they might think that's a realistic scenario. If they had actually had a bit more capital, they might have let me have another go at it! So in this dream I'd lost £862 million and Barings just said, 'That's OK, you can have another go.' I went back to Singapore. And the same thing happened all over again. I'd help hide mistakes and lose even more money. That dream reinforces for me where that line is drawn. I may be slightly frivolous looking back at some of the things that happened to me but the memory of quite how horrific they really were is never too far away to serve as a constant reminder. I don't have this dream any more. I haven't had it since I left prison. Dreams are so often hard to remember.

## IVAN

Dreaming does the emotional housecleaning for us and nature doesn't need us to remember them. It was undoubtedly about something you were going over and over in your mind and getting emotionally worked up about. Before having the dream were you thinking 'if only' thoughts?

## NICK

Possibly. I did that a lot over the years, looking at things retrospectively. I kept wondering what I would do in that same situation again. And this is where it has a spill-over effect on me, because I did wonder a lot in prison about what would happen if I had another career, another nine-to-five job, and somebody asked me to help them out and it was a little bit close to the mark? I suppose I was seeing quite how far I could push it. Perhaps the dream was a warning mechanism.

## IVAN

Were you having this dream at times when you were depressed?

## NICK

I am sure there were times when I dreamed that but I didn't get depressed for long periods and there were various methods I discovered to get out of it. Let me give you an example of the conditions that can bring on a fairly extreme depression. It's a hundred degrees in Singapore pretty much all day. Eight o'clock at night is the worst time because the heat just rises and it hits the cells. I'm in there with two other prisoners and temperatures reach a hundred and twenty degrees by the time you're trying to get to sleep. You don't have anything to cool yourself down with – there's no water, no fan or anything. You're sleeping on the concrete floor. No mattress. If the wall or floor feels a little less hot than you do you basically take the coolness out of the wall and floor into your body to cool yourself down a little. You sit or lie like that. If you're reading a book, you use the absolute minimum amount of movement to turn the page because any movement makes you sweat. It's like being in a sauna continually. You contend with that every night, sleeping on the concrete floor so you end up with boils and sores on your legs and hips, elbows and shoulders, wherever your bones rub on the floor.

**IVAN**

There were no mattresses?

**NICK**

No mattresses. I slept on a roughly finished, uneven floor. I couldn't lie on my stomach, which is the way I normally sleep. Most of the prisoners slept on their backs because, if you lie on your front, there are too many points in contact with the floor so you'd end up with boils on your knees, on your feet, on your pelvic area, your chest and chin. So it was just unbearably painful and we wouldn't sleep well at night. The sun would be streaming in by eight o'clock in the morning. The guards would come round to unlock the door and give us an hour outside where the heat was even worse – totally oppressive. You have no shoes, so you walk around in your bare feet, the heat of the floor blistering your feet as you walk. It was just the worst way imaginable to start the day. That, coupled with not knowing what was going on with my ex-wife and thinking about how many days I had left to go in that heat and confined environment. I'd be so depressed by these conditions. The heat, the fear, the worry and the uncertainty would all be bearing down on me; I've never felt worse before or after. I'd scan the cell looking for the sharpest corner that could inflict the maximum amount of damage and seriously thought about ending the pain – knocking myself out.

**IVAN**

Did you start to hallucinate or anything like that?

**NICK**

I didn't but there were plenty of people going mad around me.

**IVAN**

So what strategies did you devise to survive?

**NICK**

The most useful was that I used my mind to visualise myself away from where I was. Otherwise dwelling on the reality was so awful it would have killed me. Very often, as I went down into that yard, I'd say to myself, 'You're going down this avenue; but you can go down another one.' It was as simple as that – changing my mindset by visualising something different. I'd see other people in a trance doing the same sort of thing. They'd obviously had a miserable night and in the morning they changed those feelings by visualisation. I could also take myself away by talking to people, although there was a language barrier, of course, and by reading.

**IVAN**

They let you read books?

**NICK**

I was lucky in that I always had a fairly adequate supply of books. You're normally only allowed three a month but they tended to give me more because I'd need one a day. And one could tell whether or not I was finding the time easy to pass based on what book I was reading. I used to read Tolstoy quite often.

**IVAN**

Could you choose what books you read?

**NICK**

Friends used to send them in to me, so I had a pretty good collection. I'd read something fairly heavy if the time was passing quickly. But if it was going slow I'd read something fast-paced – action-packed thrillers mainly. Frederick Forsyth or Tom Clancy. Although I didn't really like them much, they helped me pass the time.

**IVAN**

What did you visualise?

**NICK**

Just things that were important to me, like being with Lisa. Although our relationship was based on a pack of lies, she didn't know that at the time, and there was an emotional closeness there. So, early on in my imprisonment I would visualise how we could spend time together after my release. After the divorce I focused on spending time with friends and family, my sisters, my brother.

**IVAN**

What else did you do?

**NICK**

Exercise. That was an important strategy for me. In that hour in the yard I'd just run round and round for an hour in the heat and totally exhaust myself. We were not given trainers; we ran in bare feet in a hundred degrees on the hot floor, so our feet blistered up all the time. They were raw. But you had to get used to that. The other tactic was writing. I kept a journal to give expression to my thoughts and feelings. That kept me calm. So those four things I would say were the main ways I kept myself sane – visualisation, reading, exercise and keeping a diary.

**IVAN**

What did you write?

**NICK**

Just what I was feeling. Thoughts and strange incidents would trigger it. I kept it up for four years, writing daily up to the divorce and then twice daily afterwards. I felt my writing was something for Lisa as well. It was a way of saying sorry and admitting that I'd done things wrong in the past in our relationship, never mind at Barings. It was also a reminder of how I had been in the past, how I had behaved in certain situations, how I had reacted to things, but, more importantly, how I wanted to change in the future. There wasn't much in there that was flattering – anything but. As a review of me as a person, it was all rather negative. You know, there were times when I hadn't been particularly nice to my ex-wife and could have done more for her. So I was expunging all of those thoughts and apologising. Odd things would set me off writing. We used to wash our plates in the prison yard area in a large, raised square tank full of water. Most of the time, because people dunked their plates in it, the surface was always moving and greasy. But first thing in the morning the water hadn't yet been disturbed and so was very still and calm. The sun would beat down on it and, if you looked at it in a certain way, it could remind me of a beach or some beautiful setting by water that I'd been to with Lisa when I was free. That would trigger a sense of loss, because I wasn't able to see such things locked up in Tanah Merah Prison and I would write about it – write about things that had happened during holidays I'd had and how it motivated me to want to change things in the future and be a better person and have such opportunities again. That was a strong form of idyllic visualisation that helped in the cathartic process of drawing down past experiences and feelings and being able to reappraise them. That power of reflection was with me always; of course, I had more time than most to reflect, but I'm immensely grateful that I latched on to that way of using my time. I think it was part of the remorse I was feeling.

## STRESS REDUCER

### Practise relaxation and visualisation

Taking time out of a busy life to relax every day is just about the best way to reduce the impact of stressful life events and boost the immune system. Relaxing is a natural process in which the brain 'hemispherically switches' from left-brain dominance, in which attention is primarily focused outwards on the world, to right-brain dominance where we focus inwards, reflect, daydream and integrate into our model of reality whatever recent experiences have occurred. Indeed, we are biologically programmed to do this every ninety minutes. It's an *ultradian* rhythm. Many people live such hectic, pressured lives that they override this rhythm by taking stimulants like caffeine (tea, coffee) or cigarettes. Workaholics are prime examples of people who don't relax enough and continually override this rhythm. They frequently suffer physical and mental health problems as a result. If you regard yourself as stressed or burning out, to counter the negative effects that might arise, consider incorporating some of the following into your daily or weekly routine.

- ► Establish a regular walk in a quiet, natural environment like a park or the countryside
- ► Sit beside a lake or even a pond and watch light reflecting off the water for ten minutes
- ► Swim if possible
- ► Have a massage
- ► Play a relaxation guided imagery CD
- ► Listen to music that calms you
- ► Practise deep breathing (make the out-breath last longer than the in-breath)

**IVAN**

So you kept going because you were using your imagination.

**NICK**

All of the time. But there was another thing that helped me: I had letters.

**IVAN**

Writing and receiving them?

**NICK**

I was only allowed to write two a month so I'd write one to one friend and they would send it out to ten more. It was on airmail paper folded into four pieces. I'd write to whoever I wanted to get the first bit, they would get the whole letter and then I'd say to them, can you send this bit to these people and they would post them on for me.

So I'd had a lot of letters coming in because I'd made contact, but I only had two letters I could send out.

**IVAN**

Did all the prisoners do that or did you work that system out for yourself?

**NICK**

I worked it out because I was so isolated. A lot of people didn't get letters. I was in an extremely fortunate position. I used to get between ten and fifteen letters a week for four and a half years. My survival mindset was that I had to change things to my advantage. Letters would only come on weekdays. So I didn't give myself grief about not receiving one on a Saturday or Sunday because that was self-defeating. But on a Monday I'd wake up and I'd think I've got a one in five chance of getting a letter! I used to get letters more often than anybody else. I paced the anticipation so, if I didn't receive one on the Monday, I had an increased chance on the Tuesday of receiving letters as I then had a one in four chance. And, if they still hadn't arrived, I had a one in three chance on the Wednesday. So I mentally turned things to my advantage. And they would come. Sometimes I'd get all ten or fifteen together and you'd keep them and you could reread them. They transmitted a warmth – a need that wasn't being fulfilled elsewhere.

**IVAN**

That's a really positive attitude; much better than moaning.

## NICK

Moaning wasn't going to get me anywhere; they'd all turn a deaf ear, so it would have been pointless. As frustrating as it was not to get letters every day, if I started to moan about it as well it would have compounded the problem, frustrating and stressing the life out of me. Controlling my needs was something that I had to learn. In the beginning I wanted letters every day and I would feel down when that didn't happen. I soon realised I had to be realistic. During the initial period, especially, I wanted letters from Lisa; I wrote to her every day in my journal and, rather selfishly, I thought, why can't she? But after a while they dried up. For nine months I didn't get any from her and, because I didn't know what was happening, I couldn't control my thoughts and imagined all sorts of reasons why she wasn't writing. I was having endless conversations in my head. But eventually I realised I had to stop doing that. By changing the way you think about things slightly it can have a massively beneficial influence on your life. Tweaking the way I thought about letters and communication had such an effect on me. Letters were far more important than personal visits. While visits were fantastic when people were there, they were over too soon and were sporadic at best. The letters gave me something far more regular and something to rely upon. They supported me throughout the full four and a half years of imprisonment and helped me never feel detached from society. And the diary was always there when I had no letters to answer.

**IVAN**

Did they feed you well in prison? Was it nutritious?

**NICK**

The diet was hard at first but we were fed three times a day. In the morning we were given three pieces of bread. On Monday it would have the tiniest sliver of butter or margarine on it. They might as well not have bothered! On the other days of the week we might get the smallest blob of jam you've ever seen in your life. You'd get three pieces of bread for breakfast and a cup of tea four times a week, and coffee three times a week, which was ghastly. You couldn't drink the coffee. It was hated with a passion. Coffee days were always negative days. Every day your bread was always there but if it was a tea day the prison was a little bit more cheerful than if it was a coffee day. The coffee was *so* disgusting. As soon as it was coffee day, because this was the one hot drink of the day, it put a dampener on things. Coffee was also served on the day when we used to get fish, which I also hated. I don't even know what fish it was but it was fairly small with thousands of bones and I wouldn't eat it. I just can't cope with fish and bones. The coffee days were Tuesdays, Thursdays and Sundays, which were also fish days, so the whole day was bad for me! Isn't it strange how such a minor thing can have such a large influence on your whole day – it's totally disproportionate!

**IVAN**

Life is strange. But once you've been through an experience, even one that lasted for years, it all shrinks down in memory to next to nothing, doesn't it? I bet weeks go by now when you don't even think about prison life.

## NICK

Longer even. I was in prison for four and a half years and it's five years since my release, so the periods are fairly similar. Yet my prison life seems like it never really happened. I have to work hard to remember it. With my history I can't really allow too much of my past to influence the present, other than in a positive way. The memories are still there but they are all filed away now; the positives that I have drawn from my experiences remain. My present life is very real and all encompassing. Spending too much time in the past would be denying the opportunities I've been given since my release.

## IVAN

It's like what happens when we go on holiday and it's incredibly stimulating and exciting and so much happens. But a few weeks later you're back at work and it's as if you hadn't been away at all. What other food did they give you?

## NICK

We were fed rice twice a day which, if you're used to a western diet, is difficult to cope with. I could eat it once a day but I couldn't eat it twice a day. We would have chicken three times a week, mutton three times a week and fish three times a week. And some vegetables that, if you saw them in your garden, you'd think they were weeds. So the vegetables weren't great. After I was ill they made some concessions. I used to get double meat rations and some baked beans so I could eat the rice a bit more easily. They'd also throw in some potatoes, which were unheard of in the prison. So they did look after me in that respect. I used to eat a lot of bread. Dinner would come in the evening and I'd swap it with somebody who would have kept some bread back from earlier in the day. There was a lot of smuggling going on from the kitchen because of the very strong gang culture. The gangs would send bread up to their gang members so their people would swap bread for my rice and chicken, because I couldn't eat it in the evening. So I often ate a loaf of bread a day with nothing on it. My attitude to food changed in prison and, to a certain degree, this stays with me now. Food became less for enjoyment and more of a necessity. It was something I needed to stay alive. Before prison, good, nice food, food I enjoyed, was always important to me. But now I can make do with anything. Food is what you live on, that's all it is. And, if it's nice to eat, that's a bonus. But I'm no longer one of those people who'll go to a restaurant and, if the food is not up to standard, won't eat it. I'd force it down because it's not the end of the world. I'm not going to get too political about it but there are a lot of people in the world who don't have the good fortune to eat even that prison food. I travel to Asia at least twice a year, and I've seen some of the kids in Cambodia trawling through bins to get food. The idea of complaining that the sauce on your steak might not be to the correct standard seems to me now nothing short of absurd, or even obscene.

## IVAN'S COMMENTARY

Like those of many intelligent survivors of prison life, Nick's story of incarceration gives us much to ponder. In a way it forced him to grow up and take responsibility for himself. The strategies Nick adopted to help him survive his time in an alien prison without his spirit being broken correspond remarkably to the strategies used by effective psychotherapists to combat depression.

In ordinary life depression is a signal that someone is not getting his or her emotional needs met. It is not a biological disease, nor is it caused by difficult life circumstances, as is demonstrated by the fact that for much of his incarceration Nick was not clinically depressed. It is never circumstances that cause depression but how you respond to them that matter. Depression is a very strong emotion caused by a build-up of negative expectations – worries – about the things that seem to be going wrong. These expectations trigger the autonomic arousal system that would normally act them out, a necessary process for all expectations as the cycle is completed by de-arousal. (For example, an expectation that you have to hurry to get to the shops to buy food for the evening before the shops close is de-aroused when you take the necessary action.) But, because a depressed person is *misusing their imagination* to generate an endless stream of negative expectations that they don't, or cannot, act on, at the end of each day there is an accumulation of uncompleted patterns of expectation going around in the person's head. These thoughts often make it difficult for the person to fall asleep. But, when sleep finally comes, they result in excessive, intense dreaming, particularly at the beginning of the sleep period. This upsets the balance between slow-wave, recuperative sleep and REM sleep, which is the highly active, energy-consuming state in which dreaming occurs. This is why depressed people always wake up exhausted. Moreover, because intense dreaming fires off the brain's orientation response for very long periods, they find it difficult to orientate themselves to ordinary tasks when they wake up. We need the orientation response in order to motivate ourselves to do anything. It is directly involved with the parts of the brain involved in movement and deciding to act. But the excessive intense dreaming that depressed people do, compared to non-depressed people, means their orientation response is drastically weakened when they wake up.

This latter characteristic of depressed people is why life begins to seem meaningless to them and leads to suicidal thoughts. This is because the brain gets its sense of meaning through movement – action derived from expectations. Nick, of course, was not getting all his needs met, but he did pretty well. He had strong connections to the outside world through the many letters he received which meant he felt he belonged and was valued; he had a kind of status in the prison community because of the enormity of his crime, and he was able to devise strategies that made him feel he had a degree of control over aspects of each day – such as using the washing area as a tool for visualisation. He also found humour in what was going on and kept himself preoccupied and physically fit. It is difficult to worry when you are exercising. Plus, he had reading and writing projects to keep him focused and connected and, later, when he stood up to the prison authorities over the matter of not changing his cell mates, a 'cause' that had meaning for him.

## HOW WELL ARE YOUR INNATE NEEDS BEING MET?

Nature has programmed all of us with physical and emotional needs. These are the 'human givens' that cannot be avoided. How stressed we are depends on how well they are being met now and how well we deal with situations when they are not. Rate, in your judgement, how well the following emotional needs are being met in your life now on a scale of one to seven (where one means not met at all, and seven means being very well met) by ticking the appropriate boxes.

▸ Do you feel secure?                              1  2  3  4  5  6  7

▸ Do you feel your efforts
 are appreciated?                                  1  2  3  4  5  6  7

▸ Do you think you give other
 people enough attention?                          1  2  3  4  5  6  7

▸ Do you feel in control of your life              1  2  3  4  5  6  7
 most of the time?

▸ Do you feel part of the wider                    1  2  3  4  5  6  7
 community?

▸ Can you obtain peace and                         1  2  3  4  5  6  7
 quiet when you need to?

▸ Do you have at least one                         1  2  3  4  5  6  7
 close friend?

▸ Do you have an intimate                          1  2  3  4  5  6  7
 relationship in your life
 (one where you are totally
 physically and emotionally
 accepted for who you are)?

► Do you feel an emotional
   connection to others?                   1  2  3  4  5  6  7

► Do you feel you have status that         1  2  3  4  5  6  7
   is acknowledged?

► Are you achieving things and             1  2  3  4  5  6  7
   competent in at least one
   major area of your life?

► Are you mentally and/or physically   1  2  3  4  5  6  7
   stretched in ways that give you
   a sense of meaning and purpose?

*Use this questionnaire as a guide to help you think about how your life
could be improved. If your scores are mostly low, you are more likely to be
suffering stress symptoms. If any need is scored three or less this is likely
to be a major stressor for you. Even if only one need is marked very low it
can be enough of a problem to seriously affect your mental and
emotional stability.*

## STRESS REDUCER

Try not to misuse your imagination. It is the most accessible, effective and creative tool you have for problem-solving and self-calming. And no one can take it away from you. Even if things are frantic in your life and time is at a premium, your imagination can help you to sleep and de-stress if you allow it to do its work properly. There is absolutely no point worrying about things that haven't yet happened or may never happen. One is better off nourishing oneself by nurturing a positive attitude and saving the energy required to solve real problems when they actually occur, rather than pre-exhausting yourself. Practise visualising scenarios and imagery that pleases and relaxes you – no matter how miserable your actual surroundings. Repeated visualisation can form pathways in the brain that rehearse new possibilities for our own well-being. Over time, the brain thinks we have experienced – and not just imagined – whatever images you have mentally created. Use it well.

# chapter 5
# RELATIONSHIPS,
# DIVORCE AND LOSS –
# emotions in turmoil

## NICK'S STORY

My relationship with my mother was the dominating relationship throughout my youth. I would even go so far as to say I was something of a mummy's boy, although I have always internalised my emotions, projecting a tough exterior. When my mother died, my younger sisters were ushered away from the family home to an aunt in Somerset. I was shut away in my bedroom coping with it privately, head buried in a pillow and finding it difficult to cry. Within hours I was too involved in the funeral arrangements to really finish that grieving process. To be honest, I haven't really finished it now and find it difficult to admit that I don't know how to go about it.

I never really had a chance to say goodbye to her and that hurts. I visited the hospital the evening before she died and she was in good spirits because, although she knew she was dying from cancer, she had been told that she had ten years to live – and that she would see my younger sisters through their teenage years. Unfortunately she never got that chance. She died the next morning. Not from lung cancer, as I have thought for the last fifteen years, but from a blood clot. My father finally revealed this recently when my sister began to suffer from some mild blood disorders.

Every time I go past the crematorium I want to go in, find the final resting place for my mum's ashes, tell her how much I miss her and say sorry. It is something I should have done years ago, but my sense of pride has prevented me. Part of me still finds it difficult to show the level of emotion I assume is required for such a pilgrimage. Hopefully I will make the necessary journey next time I visit the area with my wife, Leona, who has taught me how to love and trust people again, and dispel the control of this pride that overpowers me and stops me doing some things I should have done in my life – confessing at Barings included.

Throughout my life my mother was always the motivating force in anything I achieved, either academically or in business. As I mentioned at the start of this book, she always wanted a better life for her children than the one she had and, while I may have been the shining light initially, I have to think that I am the biggest failure now. My brother and sisters have gone from success to success, but I'm the one with the criminal record. I experience many contradictory feelings when I try to imagine what she would have felt, had she been alive to witness the whole media circus around the collapse of Barings. Of course I think she would have been disappointed beyond measure about what her son had got himself into. Yet the only way she was spared that disappointment was by dying before it all happened. I'd love her to be here now and for me and my family to be able to spend time with her in a more relaxed and loving manner than in my youth. I'm sure she would have forgiven me for everything that happened, but there will always be doubt in my mind.

I'd be the first to confess that my more intimate relationships to date have not been a great success. While there was always a feeling of being loved when we were younger, there were never any outward displays of affection. I can't remember our parents kissing or hugging any of the children. I don't even have memories of my youngest sister, nine years my junior, being shown close affection. And we're not much different now. Meeting up with my brother or sisters after my release from Singapore, I was more likely to be met with a handshake than a friendly kiss and a hug.

I'm sure we have adopted this cool approach, this lack of emotional closeness, from the way our parents behaved to us when we were younger. I really don't remember them being any different with each other, either. They weren't formal, as such, but somewhat distant, going about their lives without too much regard for each other. One would be reading the newspaper, the other preparing the dinner and then they'd sit in separate chairs. There was no closeness, no intimacy. You never sensed any warmth, and there was certainly no holding hands or showing affection for each other when the children were around. I knew that affection was part and parcel of many other families because I saw it at my friends' houses. I wanted my own family to be more like that and I am sure I will be very different as Mackensey starts on his path through life.

However, showing affection doesn't come as naturally to me as I would like. I've been conditioned to have different expectations for the last thirty-seven years and it's going to take a while to unlearn some of that conditioning. Not surprisingly, both of my long-term partners – Lisa and now Leona – are from families that are warm, loving, caring and supportive. It's something that I aspire to.

I'm happy to admit that my first wife Lisa piggy-backed me through those first nine months on remand at Hoechst Prison. I probably wouldn't be here today if she hadn't. Week in, week out, she would arrive with bed linen, recently perfumed that so that it smelled of her, and we would spend the stolen hour we had crying and talking over what the next week would hold for both of us. Nothing much changed in my life at that point and I thought that would include Lisa, not because it was Lisa but just because I needed something, or someone, to cling on to. But, after those initial nine months, I was thrown into emotional turmoil. The turbulence that accompanied my flight back to Singapore to face my sentencing characterised the upheaval that awaited me over the next couple of years. Despite the fact that Lisa sat next to me on the plane and consoled me into facing what lay ahead, all the positive thoughts she instilled in me about our future together were to dissipate. The collapse of the bank and of our lives must have been a harrowing experience for Lisa, and one that I can never really forgive myself for putting her through. But what I really needed at that time was a cast-iron assurance that everything would be ok. Because I had a very uncertain future. The irony was that the person who had been so dishonest over such a long period now needed honesty and security when he himself had been unable to give either.

Shortly after I was arrested Lisa was contacted by a friend from her past. After a few months they began to meet up, as friends at first, but a more intimate relationship eventually deleloped, unbeknownst to me. I was under the illusion that after all my wrongdoing there was a chance I could come through it with the thing that was most important to me at that time – Lisa. Sleep would alternate between dreams that it would happen and nightmares that it wouldn't. That chance had already evaporated, and I was the last to know it. It wasn't until August 1998, when I was lying chained to a bed in the prison ward in Changi General Hospital with the diagnosis of colon cancer running through my brain that I would learn of this turn of events.

We were just divorced by then, but my life-shattering news had upstaged her plans to remarry only ten days later. Perhaps she was genuinely worried about me, or perhaps she didn't want to detract from her special day, or possibly it was some other reason entirely. Whichever it was, she decided to postpone. I would certainly have never asked her to.

In the early days I would spend hour upon hour writing love letters to Lisa. I had never written one before but I clung on to this last desperate hope that we could salvage something. Most of the time I was saying sorry but other times I'd be trying to generate a response that would give me an insight into how she was really feeling. I'd often start by writing, I love you, I love you, I love you – a mantra that could take up half of a page. I'd write the words, but deep down I knew they conveyed a different meaning: I love myself, I love life and I need your help. The hope of a Mills and Boon ending was always at the back of my mind, unaware as I was that our very separate and distinct environments were shaping our destinies in different ways. I was being unbelievably selfish but I had to be to survive. We had had a fantastic lifestyle while we lived in Singapore but the emotional basis for our lives together had not been that strong. It was founded on my job at Barings and our life in Singapore. This was riddled with lies, and that lack of honesty certainly transferred into our private lives. While Lisa would go through her daily routine without a care in the world I would stumble into work with a false face painted on and return an empty capsule in the evening, drained of any energy or social skills that had been wrenched out of me during a day spent lying to everyone.

I'd collapse on the sofa, eat and sleep. I'd wake up at odd hours of the evening worried about something that was churning around in my head; worrying about what the markets in America were doing; worrying about being exposed for the liar I was. It is strange, looking back at that situation now, but it wasn't so very different to my life in the prison cell. Perhaps, without my realising it, the sentence had started even earlier than I remember. Looking back on my relationship with Lisa, we were initially very comfortable in many ways in terms of our views, lifestyle and future but the spark was gone almost as soon as we hit the tarmac in Singapore in April 1992. Events immediately started to take over and, once the stresses of living that huge lie overtook me, we never rediscovered the spark.

Not everything in the movie *Rogue Trader* is true to life. Anna Friel and Ewan McGregor romping their way around south-east Asia may have made entertaining viewing but it wasn't the way it was. I knew Lisa wanted a baby so that meant I ran the risk of messing up two lives; I didn't want to make it three. Therefore I ensured our sex life whittled down to nothing. Stories in the papers about my infidelities with a geisha girl are inaccurate. I do admit that during this barren period I did stray once or twice. I'm not proud of it, not proud of the manner in which it happened, but there was no pressure to be honest with this relative stranger, so it was easier than lying to my wife, whom I ran the risk of getting pregnant. A few drunken gropes in the evening, sexual satisfaction and then another lie added to the web that was constantly spreading out, growing ever wider. There was no sanctuary left; lies pervaded every inch of my life.

As I sat in the sparse prison cell that was to be my home for the next three and a half years, my thoughts would naturally return to happier times. Those memories were brief and fleeting, often triggered by the simplest thing, such as the mention in a magazine of a place we had visited together. They were quickly replaced by uncertainty and feelings of despair, the contrast between those times and my current location hitting me straight between the eyes. Not knowing what was happening, and becoming aware that the distance between myself and my loved ones was widening all the time, meant I was walking an emotional tightrope. At best I'd be managing to balance, keeping myself on an even keel but, as the uncertainty of the situation enveloped me, I would be continually plunged into the abyss of despair. I'd never been more down. The only advantage I may have had over other people in a similar situation was that I realised it. The thought of losing Lisa scared me, but more for the fact that her absence would mean there would be nothing constant in my life.

With all the uncertainty in my life I was passing from day to day in a trance. Nothing externally impacted on me. I'd run faster and longer than any of the other inmates but internally I was tearing myself apart. I'd seen many an inmate slash their wrists during my time in Germany, and I'd received a beginner's course in how to do it successfully, but the pain I was inflicting on myself internally was far more drastic – and potentially far more damaging; my emotional well-being was seriously in jeopardy. Negative thoughts flooded my mind, quickly followed by another batch of even more negative thoughts. I was eating myself up inside. There were times when I could stem the flood by exercising or reading a book, but the let-up was only temporary. Many a time I'd find myself staring up at the ceiling with a book in my lap. I'd look back at the book and realise I'd read fifty pages with no recollection of what those pages had said. My mind was tripping subconsciously over something that was worrying me and my attention was totally unfocused.

When I first arrived in Singapore I was getting regular letters from Lisa's mother, from friends who knew her and from my friends. And then, in March 1996, communication ceased completely and nobody could contact her. This contrasted painfully with the letter a day and weekly visits I'd had while on remand in Germany. Now I wasn't getting any letters from her. Every now and again I'd get a 'hi, things are fine, hope you're doing well' postcard – no emotion, no warmth in them at all – from San Francisco or whatever. It was very confusing because our relationship had, I believed, been so strong and vibrant on a daily basis. Perhaps my own need for something to hold on to blinkered me from what was really happening. I had deceived Lisa for so long – perhaps this was the result.

In the end it was me that penned the first mention of divorce. I hadn't had a letter from Lisa in months and the uncertainty was shredding my emotional well-being. My emotional and physical well-being was being very severely tested. I could be wallowing in all-consuming self-pity first thing in the morning, unable to eat, unable to wash, unable to do the simple things that kept you healthy in the prison. Other times I would be wound up so tight that another inmate even talking to me would have me screaming in his face, looking for a confrontation that neither of us really wanted. There was a limit to how far and how long this could go on. I had hit that limit. It was time to self-destruct or sort out the problems. Luckily I chose the latter. I often transported myself back to occasions when Lisa and I had been happy. This was clearly distorting any rational thinking. But during the darker moments I tried to be more objective about the situation. We had a marriage that had been put on hold for the next four and a half years, but we had little else. For the latter period of my time in Singapore there'd been little communication between us and it had been relatively empty. And I'd been unfaithful. I'd even paid a visit to my boss, Tim Easun, a month before we got married back in March 1992 and asked for a transfer overseas so that I could miss the wedding.

None of it added up to anything very concrete, and the perpetual uncertainty convinced me that I needed to change something. The situation between Lisa and me had to be consigned either to the black or to the white area; it had been grey for far too long. Divorce or dedication was the choice. Either was acceptable but I had to reclassify the situation. The months of not knowing what was going on had been torture; the next three years were going to be absolutely impossible if I didn't get it sorted out soon. So I wrote the letter offering divorce, explaining my reasons, needing to have something solid to hold on to and look forward to. I didn't think twice about sending the letter. It took me only minutes to write and it was soon off on its journey, after being scrutinised by the officers that read all my mail. She got the letter. At first she was reticent, but it wasn't too long before she agreed, and so my life would turn another corner.

## IN CONVERSATION

### IVAN

From reading your account of growing up, some people might think there is a somewhat contradictory element to the relationship you had with your mother. You describe yourself in one place as a 'mummy's boy' – which implies an overaffectionate, overprotective mother – yet you say there was no display of physical affection in your family, not even to your baby sister.

### NICK

Perhaps the description of myself as a mummy's boy is misleading. Displays of affection were very few and far between, it's true, although my mother was my favourite and I think I was probably hers. We weren't cuddling all the time and I didn't run to her with my problems every time I fell over or some other kid had roughed me up. We were all fairly able to look after ourselves and were left to our own devices most of the time. Not the classic view of a 'mummy's boy' but one that I think is still valid. My brother was a bit sportier, or at least more successful at sport, and was far better at using his hands. He would have been my father's favourite whereas my forte was my intelligence. My sisters were quite a bit younger. Personally I think how much affection a family displays is behaviour we learn during our early years. I think my parents' parents were exactly the same with them years beforehand and, as a consequence, they were just behaving in the same manner. If you don't see anything different, you don't know anything better. I've been fortunate to see an overtly loving family, and that's what I want for Mackensey, Alex and Kersty. It doesn't come naturally though; I have to make an effort.

## IVAN

There is no such thing as a 'proper' way to grieve, so why do say you have never properly grieved for your mother?

## NICK

I think it's because I always believed everything she told me. The night before she died she was told she had ten years to live. That message was passed on to me and I believed it. I went to work happy the next day and then my world fell apart when I received a phone call at work less than fourteen hours later to be told to hurry back. I never made it back in time. I failed and I was certainly in shock throughout the entire period we were making funeral arrangements. It's been such a long time since her death – seventeen years – that I'm embarrassed by the fact that I never made that effort before. That's tended to be the way I've dealt with things that have embarrassed me in the past; I avoid them. Barings and the collapse of the bank have probably been the first time I've had to face up to a situation and deal with it.

**IVAN**

It strikes me you had a pretty OK time growing up.

**NICK**

I have a lot of happy memories, more happy than bad. I may have gone a bit wayward in my teens as I wasn't achieving and therefore wasn't receiving the affection but I always did enough to pull myself through and get to the next level.

**IVAN**

You have said that the hardest part of being in prison was the divorce. Any divorce is difficult but –

**NICK**

– In prison, obviously, it's a lot more difficult. Let me try to put that comment in the correct perspective, as it's often misrepresented. Divorce wasn't the hardest thing I've encountered; it was the circumstances and manner in which it occurred that caused the greatest distress. My marriage was what I tried to hang on to. I needed something that would be there for me, no matter what; something I could rely on. It was selfish, but I needed something that I could look forward to and that could provide me with a solid base from which to move onwards through my incarceration. The realisation that this base was flimsy at best was the most difficult thing for me to cope with. I was like a small boat being tossed around in a tempest and I needed something to latch on to in order to steady myself. My marriage to Lisa fulfilled that purpose during my time on remand in Germany, but it started to founder as soon as I arrived in Singapore. I needed something definite in my life, but all I got was ambiguity. The conflict this caused in me during my time in Tanah Merah Prison was totally overwhelming. When I was in the German prison, I had dared ask myself what I would do if the roles were reversed. Would I wait four and a half years? Being honest, I didn't think I would. I visualised myself in the same dilemma, and this allowed me to rationalise that I couldn't expect anything more than I was willing to do myself. So I was quite willing to let Lisa go, to allow her to rebuild her life without me, but I needed to know which option she would choose. People fall in and out of love all of the time. We had a good relationship, but it wasn't fantastic. Often we were more like friends than partners. Putting your life on hold for four and a half years seemed a bit too much to ask of anyone. Having that understanding at the time scared me because I was desperate for something to hold on to, yet at the same time I wanted a concrete answer. I would take whatever was on offer, as long as it was definite. But her decision was out of my control. It was divorce by post in the end, which some people would think, if there were a degree of animosity between the couple, is a preferable way of doing it. But there wasn't any of that with Lisa.

## IVAN

How long had you known Lisa before you got married?

**NICK**

Two and a half years. We got married in 1992. We met through Barings and we moved out to Singapore just after we got married. Perhaps the whole marriage was founded on a bed of lies, if you like, and I think that realisation may have turned her away.

**IVAN**

The lie being the fact that when you got married you knew this financial disaster was building up?

**NICK**

Oh, no. It wasn't like that. We got married and then, about a week later, we went to Singapore. And that was my first visit to Singapore.

**IVAN**

The marriage itself wasn't based on lies, then. Prior to that you'd had a really good relationship?

**NICK**

Sure. But our life in Singapore, from fairly early on, was built upon a pack of lies. I was not the man she thought I was in terms of the business I was doing. Up until that point I had been very successful. We went out to Singapore with both of us looking forward to it, even though there wasn't a massive increase in our disposable income. In fact, I actually had a reduction in salary. We'd use up all of our disposable income every month. We couldn't save. Lisa had to work at first. She did a bit of English teaching at a local school for the first six months we were there, and we needed that income to survive. She wasn't really caught up in the story I concocted initially.

She had worked at Barings herself in England and happily socialised when people were visiting. It was only gradually that she got caught up in the success stories that were circulating at the time about me and how well I was doing. My salary was increasing; the bonuses were quite sizeable and our standard of living rapidly increased after that first nine to twelve months. Then she didn't have to work any more and her days were spent in coffee shops and in the gym and shopping. I think she grew accustomed to a better lifestyle and enjoyed the benefits of my status. Telling your wife and family that the lifestyle they are living is based on a bed of lies is one of the most difficult things to do. Even on the day Lisa and I fled Singapore, when I knew what I had done was about to be exposed, I couldn't tell her why we were leaving. I just said things like, 'There's a little problem that's got too much and I need to get out of Singapore for a while, so pack a bag; let's get away for a bit.' And she thought she would go back and pack up the rest of the belongings some other time. I just couldn't tell her that we wouldn't be doing that. As an example of quite how removed from the whole episode she was, she wanted to take two videos back to the video shop before we left Singapore. There we are with everybody hunting for me and we're taking videos back to a rental shop on the opposite side of Singapore to the airport.

**IVAN**
So she was quite unaware of the true situation?

**NICK**

Totally unaware. I now think that, when she looked back over what happened and realised that the web of lies had pervaded every part of our lives together, she quite rightly couldn't accept that. She was never influenced by what the media made up about infidelities with geisha girls in Tokyo – completely inaccurate and wrong. The journalists decided that was the reason why the divorce happened. In fact, I was living a Jekyll and Hyde type of life: on the one hand I was enmeshed in the harsh reality of the trading floor where I knew how big the losses were, and on the other I was enjoying a normal life at home with Lisa.

**IVAN**

So you dissociated yourself from the problem when you were away from work?

**NICK**

I'm not sure that it was ever out of my head completely, but I was able to shut down the situation temporarily if I was with Lisa or friends that weren't from the finance industry. If we were watching TV or out and about with friends, then there was definitely a dissociation. No one would have guessed there was anything wrong. But I could never put it totally out of my mind. We used to leave Singapore and go to different places at the weekend to relax, and that would dissociate me from the whole of Singapore – a bigger separation than being merely away from the office. But when the conversations were finished, when that need for pretence was lifted, like when we went to bed and Lisa slept, then the reality of the losses would come back to me and I'd fret badly. I couldn't sleep well. I'd be out of bed in a sort of frenzy, checking what the markets were doing on the TV. Psychologically I was in pieces. My emotional well-being was non-existent. Looking back on how I was before I moved to Singapore, how I was in the first few weeks in Singapore, and compare that with how I was behaving towards the end of my time there, there was a marked contrast that should have set alarm bells ringing. But all of them went unheeded. Stress manifests itself in a number of ways but with hindsight the most obvious must have been how my behaviour had changed.

## IVAN

Didn't she guess that something was wrong when you were doing that?

## NICK

No, she never guessed. I tried to drop a few hints, as much as anything I wanted to share some of my problems, but I always stopped short of confessing quite how bad the situation really was. She certainly never guessed how big a problem it was. Looking back I can see I was dropping clues, or at least I think I was, although they probably weren't the easiest to decipher. But I did say things like, 'I'm having a problem with one of the traders . . . he's had a few losses.' But, because I didn't quantify that in terms of the amount of money involved, Lisa didn't pick up on it. She'd worked for Barings herself so she knew what the environment was; she knew what that meant, and she knew I was taking a few risks. But, obviously, she thought I could cope and was operating within some sort of limit, some sort of constraint, but I wasn't.

**IVAN**

And everybody was telling her how wonderfully well you were doing.

**NICK**

Yes. As far as she was concerned I was extremely successful. We had a good lifestyle. Not as magnificent as the one portrayed in the movie or as some of the media reports made out, but she certainly got used to it. And I enjoyed being able to provide it. We'd go away at least once a month, sometimes more so that I could escape what was happening, but that would also have added to the aura of success. On that note, I'd rather give somebody close to me something than have it myself. I'd always want my wife or my family to have something before me. If there was an amount of money around, I'd forgo buying something for myself to give it to somebody who was special to me, if they needed it. Again I think that goes back to my childhood. My mother would always work hard to make the money go as far as it possibly could. She would rarely spend money on herself. We would all go on the school trips even though we couldn't afford family holidays. We never went abroad, for instance. I suppose that follows through even now. I get more enjoyment from giving now, whereas years ago I wouldn't necessarily have been thinking about it. I see this pattern in how my siblings behave as well, with their children. They will go without if necessary. The most demoralising thing for me when I returned from Singapore and started having a life again was waking up on the Monday morning, realising how much money I'd spent, having nothing to show for it other than a hangover and feeling totally empty. I could quite easily have hit the self-destruct button, continuing the partying, living life on the edge and ended up in the gutter. That empty feeling stopped me.

## IVAN

I think a lot of people are like that. They make sacrifices and delay gratification for people they care for, particularly children. You see the same thing with a real leader. A good general makes sure his men are fed before he feeds himself. Good parents do the same with their children.

## NICK

I'm sure I'll be that way with Mackensey and Kersty and Alex. Leona would probably say that I am already, but I was never a good general at work. I always did everything that I could for the people that worked for me, got them the best salaries, bonuses and health packages, but there was never any differentiation between me and them. I was very much one of the lads. We were all friends, and there was never any manager–employee or general–soldier relationship. That lack of role distinction backfired disastrously during my time in Singapore.

## IVAN

How was your initial relationship with Lisa after you were arrested in Germany?

## NICK

Lisa used to come and visit me in the prison once a week and we'd have 45 minutes or an hour to talk about things. She'd write most days; I'd write every day. I didn't have any restrictions in Germany on how many letters I could send. After the visits there'd be a few tears and it would be fairly emotional. But I could never convince myself that what Lisa was saying would actually happen: that we would get through it all and still be a couple at the end of it. Putting your life on hold for so long was a bit too much to ask anyone. My ensuing ill health has only ever cemented that realisation in my mind. Having that understanding at the time scared me a bit, because how could I ask somebody else to do more than I would do myself? I was desperate at that time, though, and would take whatever was on offer. I suppose a lot of the crying I did during that period was because I knew the relationship wouldn't last the prison sentence. But she was always adamant she would wait for me. Then again, people are fickle and do change their minds. She was meeting up with the man who was to become her second husband fairly soon after I was arrested.

**IVAN**

But you didn't know that?

**NICK**

I didn't. She came to visit me during the week I was going to be sentenced, but come the actual day of the sentencing she went off with friends of ours in Indonesia. I spoke to her very briefly afterwards but the next visit I had was three months down the line. Even though she had extended a holiday in Thailand for seven or ten days, she didn't come back to see me. That sent me very mixed and disturbing messages. When Lisa's letters stopped I really did beat up on myself. Her mum would write to me, but her letters didn't tell me too much about what was going on. As I was locked up for 23 hours a day, it was like my Sundays in the Frankfurt jail but seven days a week. There were always two other people in the cell but they spoke marginal English at best, so there wasn't much conversation. I couldn't have felt more alone, even though there were people with me in the cell all the time. And all I was doing was thinking about what was going on with Lisa. I needed someone to talk to, but there was no one. Writing in my diaries kept the demons at bay for a while, but there were times when I longed for interaction and would have to suppress that need, and bury it as deeply as I could. I was in that wishy-washy area I hated where I didn't know what to think because there was nothing concrete to grasp on to. There were times when I would think it was all going to work out fantastically and other times when I thought it was going to be an absolute disaster. But there was nothing definite. I would latch on to certain phrases Lisa had said and try and see hidden meanings in them. I'd get a letter from her mum and read something positive into it and then I might get something from one of my friends who said he'd been trying to call her and she wasn't answering his calls. Everything was full of contradiction. Somebody else would write and say she wasn't at the address she was supposed to be at, that she'd moved. The turmoil and stress of not knowing what she thought of me was unbelievable. I was thrown back and forth from the heights of happiness to the depths of despair. I had never been more fragile and I needed all my strength to get me through every day of the torture. Nobody could tell me what was really happening. The only definite thing in my life was the four walls of my cell, and they weren't budging. I told myself I couldn't continue as I was going. I needed to be stronger to face the years ahead and that was impossible with the uncertainty of my marriage uppermost in my mind. So I pre-empted the situation by writing a letter to Lisa saying, 'Look, if you want a divorce you can have one.' I was coming to the conclusion that the Mills and Boon ending wasn't going to happen. I needed to know one way or the other. I pointed out that I had three years left of my sentence. I explained that it wasn't going to be easy with the vagueness of the situation hanging over my head that could take me from extreme highs to extreme lows three or four times a day. I couldn't cope with the emotional turbulence caused by not knowing what was going on with her. Enduring the prison sentence was the hardest thing I've ever done in my life but the hardest part of that was the divorce. When she stopped writing letters to me I hit the most barren period of my life because I needed to focus on something positive to survive the jail term, and if it wasn't to be Lisa then I needed to find something else. I told her to make her mind up. It was all or nothing. I needed something definite. When I was diagnosed with cancer, it was at least a definite. I had a starting point. But when one is in that grey area what can one do?

## IVAN

The brain needs clear expectations to function properly.

## NICK

Exactly. My letter, although a high-risk strategy, was a positive step to bring clarity of mind. At first her reply was vague and, I thought, full of platitudes. And then a month later, after thinking about it, she opted for one. That outcome was the risk I took in writing the letter because I wasn't going to get through my sentence unless I knew how I stood.

I'd seen people in the prison yard look for the sharpest edge on the wall and run at it, splitting their head wide open. I could understand where they were coming from. You wake up in the morning to a temperature of a hundred degrees and you're sat there with nothing to look forward to and nothing to do. It's going to get worse as the day goes on and you've got a thousand or more days left to do. There were times when everything was getting on top of me but I brought myself back from the edge. I'm not silly enough to inflict pain on myself, but I got very, very close during those periods. As the prison sentence was drawing to a close I was confident I was going to finish it and that life outside would offer opportunities once more. The terrible times were earlier on in my sentence, especially when I was locked up all the time.

Once the die was cast my lawyer got to work, and about a year later brought in the decree nisi and, six months or so later, the decree absolute. But all that legal stuff didn't affect me – a decree nisi, a decree absolute – because the decision had been taken emotionally much earlier.

**IVAN**

Yes, it's the actual moment of decision that's important.

**NICK**

Exactly. My focus then changed to: 'I'm going to survive this for my family, to see my younger sisters again, to see my brother again, to see my friends.' I had relationships to move forward for. Lisa wasn't the only relationship I had and there were far more that offered stability and longevity. They were unconditional. But I did need to find that focus. From then on, whenever I had memories of Lisa, they wouldn't bother me so much. I'd write them down, get them out in the open and it would be done with, because I knew that we were never going to be a couple again. At the end of the day I'm kind of grateful for that. With all the pressures the media would have put on us when I was released from Singapore, I don't think we would have come through it anyway. But I'm not one for looking back too much at that time. I have a great life now; I have a fantastic wife and family and my friends have remained friends. Hope really does come out of adversity. When I do think back, I think of the positives, like the strength I now know I have to cope with what life can throw at me. I don't worry about the negative things that happened earlier in my life. Journalists, even now, still ask me questions about Lisa. But I've no idea what she's doing. I really don't care. She has a life of her own and I have a new life too. Mine has changed for the better and I want to make the most of it.

## IVAN

Many journalists are trained to believe that every story must have a personal case history written into it. There may be nothing inherently wrong in this but it usually overrides accuracy, facts and information. Women tend to be interested in love stories about relationships and people's lives, but men prefer the explanation, the facts, and to know what lessons can be drawn from the story. There should be a balance.

## NICK

I agree. Another thing I get asked a lot about me and Lisa, especially by Americans, is 'closure'. They seem to think we have to talk to each other to 'get closure'. But I think this is something concocted so 'closure experts' can earn a bit of money. I'm happy with the situation as it is. I don't need to speak to Lisa to achieve that, as it's already done. I don't need 'closure'. I think I can close things myself. I don't need to be in front of the person to do it.

## IVAN

There is no point in constantly going over your emotional life, revisiting it all day long, because it would drive you crazy. It causes depression. It is interesting to look at statistics here. Roughly two to three times more women suffer from depression than men. I think this may be because women are more disposed to emotional introspection than men.

## NICK

I think the male approach is a very effective coping mechanism. I'm sure that there are certain people who would like me to start every day feeling negative about everything that happened to me, especially what happened at the bank. I've been remorseful; nobody is more sorry than I am for what happened, but I refuse to go over it again and again for the rest of my life. I've been given a second chance for lots of very different reasons and I won't weigh myself down with the baggage of that period for the rest of my life. Introspection is fine, but I had nearly five years for that, every day spent in a very small cell. Ultimately you have to reach a point where you move on and leave that baggage in the past.

## IVAN

I think evolution is driving us to be less emotional. That's why the higher cortex evolved, to damp down our emotions and get us to think beyond the immediate moment and look at more options. When we just react emotionally we are reverting to an animal state; we lose our humanity and close the door on other options. One cannot see the bigger picture when one is highly emotional because strong emotions focus and lock our attention mechanism. A big advantage men have over women is that they practise, from an early age, suppressing their emotions. They have to, otherwise they would be more easily overwhelmed by them and unable to think straight. There was a popular notion circulating a few years ago, probably when you were in prison, that 'men should get more in touch with their emotions'. It was highly dangerous. What is needed is *understanding* about emotions and the different ways men and women evolved to deal with them. It's going against evolution and nature to encourage men to get more emotional. We've spent millions of years trying to put a lid on emotions! It's when men get really emotional that they tend to do the most damage.

## NICK

I agree with you. Looking at my actions in Singapore, I was on an emotional rollercoaster. There were good days and bad days where I would seesaw from the most magnificent highs to the most depressing lows. I think I was more driven by emotion throughout the whole period in Singapore than any sort of rational thought.

**IVAN**

When men lose it emotionally, they are more likely to take extreme actions.

**NICK**

I agree with you entirely. Everybody has rows from time to time, and I'm not going to deny that I don't get into arguments, but that is always the time when I behave at my most inappropriate, say what I don't really mean, and hurt people. I suffer pain for a long time afterwards. I tend to keep quiet as much as I can but when I can't keep that up any more the resulting outburst has so much more venom and force.

**IVAN**

The problem is that, when a woman becomes emotional, she wants to talk, shout, cry and express herself. Men, on average, when things are getting difficult, go the opposite way. They just want to walk away, leave the situation and calm down. And that's a perfectly sensible and proper strategy for them. But it drives women crazy, and in a way it's unfair on women because they have a need to unload. But if a man stays put, emoting, his blood pressure shoots up and he's in danger of having a heart attack. He knows he's going to become stupid and he might say or do something he's going to regret for ever. It's a no-win situation.

**NICK**

I don't row often, but if I do I can be the biggest idiot I know, in terms of what I say and do.

### IVAN

Research shows that boys are more sensitive to emotional disturbance than girls. You'll find this as your son grows up. One research project about this had small children, boys and girls, playing in a nursery. Over a loudspeaker came the sound of a baby crying in great distress. It was a recording, but of genuine distress. The children had previously been taught that they could turn the speaker on and off. And all the little girls were going, 'Oh dear, poor baby, perhaps we ought to tell the teacher,' and that kind of stuff. After a short while, the boys couldn't stand it any longer. They just walked over and turned the sound off. And the researchers at first thought that meant boys are insensitive. But, when they monitored the children, they found that the boys' cortisol levels, blood pressure, heartbeat and everything were shooting up really high. They were physiologically and psychologically *more* distressed than the girls. So boys are more sensitive to high emotions than girls, and that's why they work hard to turn them down.

### NICK

But that goes against the sentimental idea that posits emotional arousal is usually a good thing and that women are better with emotions than men.

### IVAN

It's not quite as straightforward as that. Women need to be more tuned into their emotions than men because they are usually the ones who bring up children. They are interested in the workings of relationships more than men and are more sensitive to emotional nuances. But human beings, as a species, need the ability *not* to get hijacked by emotions, because strong emotions stop thought. We should never forget that the handmaiden of all tyranny is emotional arousal. When it is abused by anyone in a position of power, it is a controlling system that can make the person on the receiving end feel debilitated and depressed.

## STRESS REDUCER

**Always remember: strong emotions make us stupid**
Never forget that there is a direct link between the level of emotional arousal and intelligence. Strong emotions have their place in emergencies and for survival purposes, such as when we legitimately need to get angry to defend ourselves or fall in love to procreate, but tend to get in the way elsewhere in our lives because they narrow down our attention too much. The rule is: the more emotionally aroused we are, whatever the emotion – pleasant or unpleasant – the more simple-minded we are.

## STRESS REDUCER

### Become aware of the connection between tyranny and emotional arousal

A person who likes to get their own way invariably hits on the tactic of getting emotional to make the other person back down. Tyranny uses oversimplification to stop thought. Therefore, because strong emotions inhibit thinking, tyranny's handmaiden is emotional arousal. This is a common source of severe distress for people on the receiving end.

In essence a tyrant is saying, 'Don't think about it, do what I want!' That is why raising the emotional temperature in this way is so dangerous. Conditioning relies on raising people's emotions before implanting beliefs. And brainwashing too. In no time induced fear can reduce a person to little more than a cowering animal.

Everyone is capable of being tyrannical and only by understanding the way tyranny works within our own minds, as well as the minds of those we live and work with, can we free ourselves from it and see how it works on a larger scale – in organisations and governments, for example.

The traditional tyrant typically uses bullying, threats and fear to crush opposition. Tyrants exist in marriages, schools, businesses, religious institutions and government departments. Many of them would also be classed as social psychopaths. One study found that one in six male managers displays behaviour that can be so categorised.

Excessive criticism and overprotectiveness, whether projected at an individual or a whole population, are also tyrannical behaviours.

## STRESS REDUCER

**Become more aware of emotional manipulation**
It is the human proneness to fear that makes us susceptible to manipulation. Fear and emotional arousal is used by people in relationships to control their partners or children. And when those with power are tyrants – whether politicians, bureaucrats, businessmen, religious despots – they use fear to control people. It is the antithesis of worthy behaviour, whatever guise it takes. We cannot operate effectively when we are afraid. So why be afraid?

**NICK**

You're so right. People need to understand, given the high rate of marriage break-ups, how men and women respond to emotional arousal in different ways. I certainly always want to avoid emotional encounters and get out of there, but my wife will always want to talk. I forget how many times I've been woken up at one or two in the morning to talk about something that has been bothering her during the day. Being in prison, having to cope with the emotional disturbance of that divorce, cancer and coming to terms with what I had done at Barings, made me realise that it's pointless to ignore those emotions: they have to be dealt with. If you can't or don't want to talk about them, writing them down can be just as therapeutic. It certainly kept me on an even keel during my incarceration.

**IVAN**

I bet your first thought when things started to go wrong at Barings was not 'I must find someone to talk to about my feelings of panic.' Your instinct was to keep a lid on it.

**NICK**

Oh yes. I feared that if I had told Lisa about it she would have told *everybody* immediately. But maybe putting a lid on it was a big disadvantage in this instance. I became very stressed out, took more risks and, although I never set out to deceive people, ended up lying to everyone. I always expected to be found out eventually, from day one. But keeping a lid on my emotions, not being able to share them with anyone, allowed me to go from day to day, whereas if I'd been totally emotionally aroused at the time and, at this emotional peak, had a frenetic day of trading, lost a lot of money – but considerably less than the £862 million I did – Barings would still be around.

## IVAN

It comes back to balance, doesn't it? I mean, the stiff-upper-lip tradition is great up to a point, but it can also produce cruelty. The strategy, when something happens, to wait and see and not just react in an emotionally driven way is a big evolutionary advance. But there are times when we should react immediately and be driven by emotions, like when defending ourselves or averting some disaster.

## NICK

That's right, but the stiff upper lip served me well in other situations such as when I was diagnosed with cancer. It's about applying the correct coping mechanism to the situation. But what you've said makes me wonder, could there ever be a female rogue trader? There hasn't been one that I'm aware of to date.

## IVAN

Well, women aren't generally such risk-takers as men. And, because they are more concerned about relationships than men, the thought of what would happen if someone were to find out is more likely to stop them, so they would never let it get that far. When you think about it, nearly all major criminals have been men.

## NICK

You're probably right. They'd all be more inclined to talk about it also. Certainly all the financial scandals I'm aware of principally involve men: Robert Maxwell,

Peabody and Co., Kenneth Lay at Enron, Conrad Black at Hollinger International …

**IVAN**

A woman may go along with a man who's taking big risks, including lawbreaking. But I suspect women don't often initiate events.

**NICK**

I think you're right. There will probably never be a female rogue trader, although there are a lot of women in the financial sector doing very well. They can be ruthless and successful.

**IVAN**

Was your relationship with Lisa changed by the stress you were under after you opened the 88888 account?

**NICK**

Yes – when the losses started to come on board in the 88888 account and I was trying to avoid the attention of all the people who were supposed to be controlling me. Once my stress levels rose I don't think there was the closeness that there'd been before. I was too stressed out for much of that. All I wanted from home life was to be safe and we mainly watched TV from our sofa or went to the cinema or planned weekend trips away. But it wasn't safe when we were in the bedroom. The sexual part of our relationship dripped down to virtually nothing. If you look at it chronologically, at the end of 1992 I'm going to get a slap on the wrist; at the end of 1993 I'm probably going to lose my job; at the end of 1994 I'm going to jail. So the last thing that I needed was a child. I was very clear in my mind about this at the time. So Lisa's emotional needs were not being met.

**IVAN**

So she wanted a baby?

**NICK**

Definitely. But that was the last thing I wanted because, in my heart of hearts, I knew how bad everything was. The losses were mounting, over $100 million, and the pressure was increasing. If we had a baby it would unfairly attach Lisa to me when or if I was imprisoned. Being in prison for a number of years and not seeing my child grow up would have been my worst nightmare. I suppose that led to a lot of dissatisfaction for her, but it was a necessary thing for me. Looking back at that period, I think I was totally emotionally dissociated with what was happening in our relationship. That really has only been rekindled since meeting Leona. So neither her nor my emotional or sexual needs were being met at that time because I couldn't let them be. So I was certainly dysfunctional in that respect.

**IVAN**

Stress has a big impact on the sex drive at any age.

**NICK**

So does drinking too much. I used to come home on a Friday night, get completely drunk, same again on Saturday. I had a lot of blackouts. We'd go out drinking with friends, large groups of us. At two o'clock in the morning Lisa would want to go home and I'd stay on with the boys and be totally paralytic when I arrived home.

When I'd wake up the following afternoon I'd have very little recollection of what had happened. I would flinch a bit at the thought of what I might have got up to. Looking back, it's so different to the way I am now. I do still go out and like to have a drink but just not to the extremes I was doing then. I'm very mindful of drinking too much. Health is very important to me now.

**IVAN**

Did you reflect in prison on how your drunkenness affected Lisa?

**NICK**

Going home on her own while I stayed on and got blind drunk was miserable for her. I was trying to blot out the reality of what was happening at the bank, but she didn't know that. So I was avoiding things during that period, sex being one of them. So I resolved to be more attentive in any future relationship. Lisa had emotional needs for attention and closeness, as my wife does now, and I didn't meet them. I think people need to be more aware that, if emotional needs aren't being met, then that's where the problem is. All things start to go wrong from there. It's a simple equation when you think about it, and it's only in your *Human Givens* book that it's so clearly said. It made me think deeply about it. I'll admit to you now that I probably don't satisfy Leona's emotional needs as much as I should, but your book has prompted me to be more aware of that and to try to make sure I do. But I'm very conscious of the fact that's it's a two-way flow as well. I'm one of these people who finds it difficult to give affection unless I'm receiving it. And I get into an awful conundrum. Who's going to be the first one to start? From a woman's perspective, at any age she has a need to be told she looks good and to be treated affectionately. But, from a man's perspective, I'm not really too worried that I'm a bald, 37-year-old who's carrying a little too much weight. I don't need to be told I look good because I wouldn't believe it anyway. But I do need affection and to feel valued for myself. But the puzzle to me is who makes that first move? I don't know if other people feel this. I'm sure I'm not unique. Is one able to meet another person's needs if one's own needs are not met? Where does it start?

## IVAN

It starts earlier with both men and women having greater knowledge of this whole thing about needs. It has to start when we are young. One of the needs in a relationship is that people have to feel valued by the other person and the normal way that happens is through affection and tolerance of minor misdemeanours and idiosyncratic behaviours. People should also have more awareness that the needs are different between the sexes. When women get upset or emotional, for example, they tend to prefer talking about it and men don't because it damages them to do so. When women express emotions it tends to calm them down, so the feelings blow over quickly, unlike male emotional turmoil which tends to last longer and be more damaging to their physiology. Men tend to bottle up their emotions, because it's a good survival strategy. Problems can arise when one person in a relationship thinks that getting emotional is a good way to resolve something. In fact, if one half of the partnership adopts

IMPROVING RELATIONSHIPS ▶

this strategy too often, he or she becomes a tyrant and such behaviour tends to drive the other person further away. Another difference in relationships is that men tend to *distrust* emotions whereas women tend to *trust* them. That major difference between the sexes can cause tremendous confusion.

**NICK**

That's the whole thing about being different. We have to practise tolerance and understanding.

**IMPROVING RELATIONSHIPS**

**The Four Destroyers of Relationships**
- Criticism
- Defensiveness
- Contempt
- Withdrawal

The American psychologist John Gottman found that marriages/relationships that succeed have to feature conversations that overcome the 5/1 rule: for every hour of interaction where at least one partner is critical, defensive, contemptuous or withdraws from engaging with the other, at least five hours of positive communication must take place.

When couples argue it is more common for the man to be defensive or to withdraw.

# IVAN'S THOUGHTS ON EMOTIONS

## WHY MEN TEND TO SUPPRESS EMOTIONS

Nick's behaviour in avoiding the emotional scenes that would inevitably occur if he revealed what was really going on, and how panicky he felt, is typical male behaviour. From a very young age boys are more emotional than girls. This is easy to confirm from personal experience. When families break up, for example, it is boys who are most emotionally disturbed by arguing parents and divorce. Boys are also more distressed by a family bereavement. In all kinds of situations, it is boys and men who feel the most intense emotions and are more physically damaged by them: they are prone to increases in heart-rate, rises in blood pressure, problems with the immune system etc. This difference seems to occur because the male autonomic nervous system, which largely controls the body's stress response, is more sensitive than the female's and takes far longer to recover from emotional upset. Because of this, males have evolved ways to suppress or override emotions. And in this they are encouraged by parents and wider society, which bring to bear social pressure to encourage restraint, thus keeping their attention off their emotions and focused outwards.

Girls, on the other hand, because they are less emotionally intense at a young age, are allowed, and indeed encouraged, to express their emotions. This difference between the sexes, with men on the whole more skilled in controlling and holding back emotions and women more skilled at expressing and putting emotions into words, is at the root of much contemporary marital conflict.

IMPROVING RELATIONSHIPS ◀

The fact that, in arguments, male blood pressure and heartrates rise significantly higher than rates in females, and stay higher for much longer, is at the root of why a man typically prefers to stonewall or withdraw when his female partner is upset about something. Men stay silent or leave the room because they are trying desperately to keep a lid on emotional arousal. They have learned that, if they were to verbalise their feelings and get angry, they would lose control of the ability to think straight; their blood pressure would go up even more; and they would put themselves in danger of having a heart attack or even becoming violent in a crude attempt to resolve their distress. But, because women have an equal need to do exactly the opposite and so want to express their feelings, this typical male behaviour winds them up and a spiral of misunderstanding can easily develop.

## ASSESSING THE STRESS LEVEL – HIGH OR LOW – IN YOUR RELATIONSHIP

Nick did not discuss with his first wife the difficulties he was getting into at work and the fact that he was not the successful young trader he appeared to be. Ultimately this led to the collapse of his marriage. Relationships and marriages are breaking down faster than ever, resulting in increased stress levels among vast numbers of adults and children.

### The starting point
All couples have problems that can raise stress levels in either partner and trigger so much emotion that they can't think straight. Invariably these problems are due to three things:

- ► Emotional or physical needs not being met
- ► Social conditioning that has created unrealistic expectations of the relationship
- ► Lack of understanding about the differences in the male and female approaches to thinking and emotions

Having a good relationship depends on being able to work together as a team to solve problems in a state of reduced emotional arousal.

It is vital to take time to talk about and come to understand the real concerns you both have *before* seeking solutions to the problems. Don't rush this step, however upset one of you may be.

**Charting relationship problem areas**

The following is a simple but effective measure of common problem areas in relationships. The list simply contains a list of issues most of which, sooner or later, all couples have to deal with. Make two copies of this list on separate pieces of paper so that you can each fill out your own one independently.

Working separately, rate how much of a problem each area currently is in your relationship: write down a number from zero (not at all a problem) to ten (a severe problem) next to each area. For example, if children are a moderate source of conflict, you might write five next to Children. If children are not a source of conflict in your relationship, you would enter a zero next to Children. If children are a severe source of conflict, you might write ten. Feel free to add other areas not included in our list. Be sure to rate all areas.

- Security, safety
- Autonomy and control
- Attention (giving or receiving it)
- Friendships
- Emotional connection
- Being part of the wider community
- Status – recognition
- Sense of achievement
- Meaning (being stretched)
- Money
- Recreation, fun
- Jealousy
- Career/work
- In-laws (or other relatives)
- Alcohol/drugs or other addiction
- Sex
- Children (or potential children)
- Religion
- Regular household jobs
- Spending quality time together
- Other

**HOW TO USE THIS LIST**

If you are dealing with real problems in your relationship, the likelihood of conflict is high. The following procedure is designed to minimise the chances of this happening. But you both need to follow the procedure sincerely.

1 After completing the above list set aside time to discuss the problems it raised. Don't get emotional and really listen to what each other is saying and check back that

you understand exactly what each other is referring to under each heading.

2 Between you, construct a list of those problem areas in which you both rated the problem as being *less* serious. These are the problem areas you can use to practise this approach: dealing with specific problems with specific solutions. This will increase your skills and give you more confidence when it comes to the bigger issues facing the relationship.

3 Set time aside regularly to work through the list, approaching the more difficult areas as you succeed with the less serious ones.

### DISCUSSING THE PROBLEM – THE RULES

▸ There must be an atmosphere of acceptance and mutual respect at the time of discussion.

▸ When one person is talking the other person listens and does not interrupt, however much they disagree. (This is not easy for most people, because of the strong emotions involved, and is one of the main reasons why a neutral third party is useful to act as a mediator.)

▸ Each of you must be clear and concrete about what you are upset about.

▸ Do not move on until each of you has said what you want to say and the other person has acknowledged it by summarising the other person's position back to them. (This is the skill known in diplomacy and psychotherapy as 'active listening'. If you do it well, progress is often swift.)

▸ Use 'I' statements to explain your position. In other words, focus on how a problem situation makes you feel rather than on projecting blame. This, as well as being specific in dealing with actual behaviour and events, avoids the tendency to character assassinate the other person's personality, which is guaranteed to cause them to become defensive and withdraw or attack you back.

**SOLVING THE PROBLEM**

- ► At each discussion agree precisely on what you are going to focus on. Don't jump about from topic to topic.
- ► If appropriate, break the problem down into smaller chunks.
- ► Brainstorm possible solutions. Any idea, however off the wall, is OK to suggest because you never know where it might lead. Although one of you writes the separate ideas down you must both generate the solutions together.
- ► Don't pass judgement on ideas that come up during brainstorming, verbally or non-verbally (such as by pulling a sarcastic face!).
- ► Be as creative as you can. And laugh if you can. Bringing a sense of humour to the situation usually helps enormously.
- ► When you find a solution you can both agree on, even if this involves a degree of compromise, go for it. Create a plan of action and agree to stick to it.
- ► Remember that no one has a great marriage or relationship if one person insists on getting their own way all the time. So be prepared to compromise to some degree. (All successful human relationships involve compromise.) To nurture a relationship requires both parties to put the needs of each other above their own a good part of the time.
- ► Follow up later to see how well your plan of action is working.

# chapter 6
## CANCER – from diagnosis to recovery

## NICK'S STORY

I awoke shackled just above my ankle to a bed on an operating table in New Changi Hospital with a vague recollection of a doctor having said the word 'cancer' to me. As I struggled back to consciousness from the fuzzy world of the anaesthetic that had preceded the endoscopy, I was greeted by a kaleidoscope of colours on the monitor. At any other time this splash of colour would have been welcome; life had been a drudgery of the greys and whites of prison walls for the last three and a half years, so any bright visuals relieved the monotony. But not these. Not this time.

A nurse busied herself around the beds of the other inmates, trying to avoid their glazed stares or expectant glances that would invite her to embark on a conversation that would be barked down by the guards. The metal manacle attached to my leg scraped along the bed protector as I dragged myself to a semi-recumbent position. From this point I could at least reappraise any changes that might have occurred to the prison ward since I had been in the civilian part of the hospital. Not that I'd looked like any other civilian as I'd been brought there, shackled hand and foot and staggering through the growing throng of interested onlookers. White-collar crime is severely frowned upon in the Far East, and they'd all been eager to get a look at the notorious patient being frog-marched through the hospital.

The impregnable steel-encased double doors still remained at the front of the prison ward building; the commando guards still had guns. No one was allowed to talk and, if you wanted to go to the toilet, you had to put your hand in the air and hope that a guard could be bothered to unchain you. It was either that or the indignity of forcing yourself up on to your knees to urinate in full view of the rest of the ward. So nothing had changed.

The official line was that the heavy security was designed to protect the outside world against the chance of any of the inmates escaping. In reality it was keeping one of the most diverse collection of illnesses ever housed in one ward from the gaze of normal society. There were inmates with tuberculosis; there was an impressive array of tropical diseases, and the guys on either side of my bed had AIDS. None of them was much of a risk to anyone as they lay there contemplating their chances of survival and trying to get from day to day with the minimum of discomfort. Add my cancer to the list and you probably had the most deadly collection of illnesses in the world nestled among those fifteen beds.

Since I'd been in the prison I'd always tried to find a positive thought, however small, to keep me going. They weren't many in number but I sincerely believed that, if the collapse of the bank hadn't happened when it did, I was fast-tracked towards a heart attack and an early grave. The late nights, the excessive drinking, the fine wine and foods, along with all the stress I was under, was a recipe for disaster. There'll probably be a few who think that was the least I deserved, but I didn't dwell on that, and instead took some solace in the fact that the bank's collapse had probably averted my dying of heart failure in my early thirties. All of the same factors had, however, contributed to the cancer that I was now diagnosed with. You don't get cancer at 31 years of age, or at least I didn't think you did.

Cancer is common enough, with one in three people being diagnosed with the disease during their lifetime. I consider myself a reasonably educated person but my knowledge of cancer at the time of my diagnosis was extremely limited. Cancer meant only one thing to me then: death. My mother had died of lung cancer just over ten years earlier, so the subject had a connotation that I neither wanted to comprehend nor find out anything more about. My mother had been told she would live for ten years but, in fact, was robbed of her life within 24 hours of the diagnosis. These shocks and extremes were what I associated with cancer. But my fears were very indicative of the collective fear that we in western society have about the disease. My survival – even in the harshest of circumstances – proves that those fears need to be alleviated.

I had felt an immense sense of loss for my mother at the time of her death but I found, immediately following my diagnosis, that I was missing her terribly again. We'd never had the chance to say goodbye as her end had been so sudden, but I found myself now seeking that chance, and wanting to ask her some questions, to find out more about the illness that had taken her and was now challenging me. I was confused. I didn't understand the diagnosis. I'm not even sure there had properly been one. I was playing devil's advocate in my mind and fearing the worst, but no doctor had really explained the situation to me. I was frightened by the lack of information. Was I going to die? If so, when? How would I die and in how much pain would I be? All of these thoughts catapulted themselves around my head looking for answers. But I had none to give.

My confusion and worry was typical of the standard reaction for any person diagnosed with a life-threatening illness. In the clinical reality of a prison hospital the medical staff was inclined to give only the simplest technical facts about the disease. Yet I was desperate for information and support. When the doctor did finally arrive and tell me that there was a malignant tumour in my colon, and that it would need to be removed, I pushed him on my chances of survival. I was told that I had a 60 per cent chance of five-year survival. Perhaps I was knocked a bit sideways by this, but surely he could have found a better way of supplying a diagnosis.

Did this mean I was going to live for only five years? Did it mean I wasn't going to live even that long? And what would happen after the five years were up? In my confused and frightened frame of mind, his statement was providing more questions than answers, and was muddying the picture even further. Unfortunately this type of prognosis is based upon the amount of time that an 'average person' with the condition might be expected to survive. Furthermore, it is usually based on the medical treatment that is available when a significant body of research into the disease takes place. As this can be made several years prior to a person's diagnosis, it is difficult to be accurate and, therefore, not that useful. I received my bad news in unusually harsh circumstances, but even in hospitals in Britain patients are given the bad news about their possible life expectancy in ways that magnify the emotional factors already playing havoc in their minds.

Back in New Changi Hospital, I needed to change my frame of mind, but there was no one I could talk with. I was surrounded by people who had possible death sentences of their own hanging over them and others who, if they survived, had another twenty or so years left to serve in prison. They were hardly going to be upbeat and a positive influence on me. I wasn't seeking sympathy; I was seeking knowledge. I don't really look on sympathy as a very useful tool. When my mother died, most of the phone calls I received with words of condolence and sympathy had me breaking down. As well meaning as the words were, they didn't help me. For me, dwelling on the emotional aspects of an event tends to compound a situation rather than relieve it.

My ex-wife actually postponed her wedding after she heard of my illness. My first thought was, what on earth for? It didn't make me feel any better. Chained to my bed there wasn't much I could do to communicate with my friends and family. The prison authorities had pretty much imposed a blanket media ban on all communications until they had a better handle on my situation and that meant they had taken away my privilege of writing letters to family and friends. The consul from the British Embassy and my lawyer, Stephen Pollard, became the conduit for all communications. I received numerous letters of support very quickly after the diagnosis and they were all gratefully received but I needed to be doing something constructive. Wallowing in my bed feeling sorry for myself really wasn't cutting it.

I was a young man chained to a bed in a prison ward with potentially very little time left to live. I wanted to get out of that hell-hole and as quickly as possible. There was an obvious focus for my thoughts and actions, one that is not usually open to someone just diagnosed with cancer, but I appealed for an early release from my sentence. My hopes were quickly dashed in a number of days by the Singaporean authorities. My lawyers, in conjunction with the help of the British High Commission, had made the necessary representations but they had all fallen on deaf ears. Rather than feeling totally crestfallen by this news, I had used the intervening period of waiting for their decision as a time of information-gathering that was going to prove priceless in my ongoing battle with the disease. A close friend had sent me a book entitled *Everything You Need to Know About Colon Cancer*. While it had lain gathering dust for a couple of days, not being the most appealing reading material for someone more drawn to blockbusting thrillers, I found with increasing urgency that I wanted to know more and more about the disease that afflicted me.

I cannot underestimate the benefit this book had on me; and I would say that it is essential, if you have been diagnosed with a life-threatening illness, that you read as much as you can and take on board the facts in order to dispel some of the myths you may have absorbed about cancer from first-hand experience and through the media.

The most important of these is that it is clearly possible to survive and go permanently into remission from cancer. Death isn't necessarily the inevitable outcome. Remission was my target and it fed my hunger for more information. None of this is obvious when you are first diagnosed with the disease. It was only through starting on a journey, a new learning curve, that this knowledge started to give me hope and enable me to think more positively about my situation. Empowering myself with this information put me at the centre of my own healing process. I suddenly had questions for the specialists that I would never have dreamed of asking beforehand and I had a thirst for knowledge about my condition. I was not going to be a passive patient; I wanted wholeheartedly to be as pro-active as possible in recovering my health.

Nearly 300,000 people per year in the United Kingdom receive a diagnosis of primary cancer, while a similar total receive a re-diagnosis of secondary cancer. Obviously this is something that we all dread, but I know from my own experiences that there are many ways of forestalling that fateful day. As worried as you may be about picking up an information leaflet today and learning something about cancer, that information is going to equip you with the tools to react better to any sign or symptom of the disease that you may experience in the future. I spent a month in solitary confinement in Tanah Merah Prison, during which time several symptoms of cancer developed. While I would never want to repeat any of my experiences in Singapore, my time in solitary was definitely the hardest period. I was locked up for 24 hours a day for over a month with the lights switched on at night and off during the day. My food was delivered through a cat-flap in the door. During my time there I suffered substantial weight loss and developed diarrhoea that was rapidly to become chronic. I put this down to the constant strain and stress that I was under in solitary confinement and didn't bother making a referral to the doctor.

A lot of people, when faced with a possible symptom of cancer or cancer recurrence, will deliberately put off that visit to the doctor, leaving themselves in a state of limbo where they don't know if anything serious is wrong, hoping that it will go away. It won't! Prevention really is the best cure through early treatment of both the symptoms and the disease. Putting off going for a diagnosis as I had meant I had lost the opportunity to treat the cancer in its early, curable stages.

The doctor I initially saw told me the dizziness I was experiencing was due to the fact that I was getting old, which seemed far too glib an analysis, yet I didn't say as much. My haemoglobin levels were dropping on a monthly basis but I never thought to ask why. The diarrhoea passed from a second, into a third and fourth month but still I couldn't muster a question. I was a totally passive patient and did everything the doctor requested without one query passing my lips. It wasn't until the fifth month of iron tablets – and the associated stomach cramps that went with them – that I finally did something. I returned all my medication, told them that it wasn't working and put the ball back in their court. I was conscious of the signals that my body was sending me but was totally ignorant of what they were saying. It wasn't that I was in denial of what was happening to me but rather that I had complete faith in the acumen of the doctor. In my case this was misplaced.

My preoccupation with being released from my sentence served me well in the first few days after diagnosis. I resented the fact this had happened to me while I was in a Singaporean prison and removed from all of my friends and family who could support me through this desperate period of my life. While I did grieve at the thought that I may die, I had not had the sense of a certain future for a number of years, and had never really acknowledged the depressed state I was in. Looking back at the situation, I think that I was at the eye of the hurricane. Relatives, friends, even lawyers that were just a little bit away from the centre of that storm were being thrown around wildly by the shocking changes to my health. I was strangely calm and stoical, however. I had nobody to confide in so there were none of those awkward pregnant pauses that can ensue when you are briefing some-one of a difficult situation for the first time. Telling people about my fate and diagnosis was probably the thing that worried me most immediately, but even that trauma was removed from me by the British Embassy. After all the uncertainty that had torn away at my insides after waking from the anaesthetic, I began to feel strangely at peace with the reality of the situation. I'd be lying if I said the reality did-n't scare me – it did and it still does to this day – but I began to experience a strange tranquillity that I could face this, backed up, of course, with a large dose of Leeson stubbornness.

People will react to a diagnosis of cancer in a number of ways: with fighting spirit, taking an active stand against the cancer, believing fully that you can affect your own survival; with denial, by pretending to yourself and others that there is nothing seriously wrong; by being fatalistic, becoming resigned to what is happening, or by becoming anxiously preoccupied by helplessness and hopelessness. I chose the route of the fighting spirit but, in the initial phases, this was more by luck than judgement. I'd been stuck in an Asian prison full of triad gangs for the last three years, and the Asian concept of 'not losing face' stood at the forefront of every inmate's daily mantra.

There were times I laughed at it; it seemed ridiculous. For instance, when the An Soong Tiong triad were planning a gang clash with the Omega gang, everyone would have to turn up for fear of looking weak. The clash would occur, last about two minutes and then the guards would quickly and violently quash it, packing the majority of the participants off to the punishment cells for another round of mental and physical torture. Why they bothered was beyond me, as nothing ever changed. But that stoic determination in the face of adversity was my spur; and now it was me against everyone who doubted I could get through this next chapter of my troubled existence. Sympathy was OK in small doses from the right people, but a show of compassion from a prison warder or my ex-wife didn't really cut much ice with me. If anything, I wanted to show them that their compassion was misplaced or mistimed, and that I could overcome my misfortune on my own terms and emerge stronger for the experience.

The Asian concept of not losing face was propelling me to present a stronger front to everyone. Sure, there were times when I wanted to cry and let the wealth of emotional backlog overflow, but that's not the way you survive an Asian prison, and that was always at the front of my mind. After all, there'd been enough crying in Germany before I'd been sent back to Singapore and it had never improved my mindset then, so it was unlikely to do me any good now. In my case, presenting a strong face didn't mean walking around with a permanent smile; having a fighting spirit meant being able to face reality and give the appropriate emotional responses. I felt it more as a bottoming out of my feelings, followed by the need to set about gathering the necessary information to mount a realistic, pro-active response to the situation. If I needed to express my feelings, the safest and most successful way for me to do that was to keep a diary of what I was experiencing.

I have been characterised in some of the more accomplished English newspapers as a robot, or emotionally barren, but that was a necessity for that period in my life. One cannot fight a battle with one's emotions running riot. The rationality and level-headedness that I now possess is a direct result of some of the experiences I had at this time. Discovering the meaning of life is something I'd always left to Monty Python, but for the first time in my life I began to have thoughts about what it would be like to die. I still don't know the answer, and I hope it is something I can postpone for a long while, but it occupies your mind after a diagnosis of a life-threatening illness. I found that I corresponded with people I knew vaguely but not well on this topic. I never broached the subject with the people who were closest to me. In fact, I never have to this day, and I don't feel that decision has worked against me. I have male friends as well who are struggling in their own ways with different illnesses but talking to each other about it is probably the last thought in our minds. It's a very male thing; I think two women would confide in each other far more quickly, or a woman and a man, but put two men together to talk about their problems and it usually results in a stony silence. I'm more inclined to talk about it now than ever before but you still sense the unease among male friends that I may talk to about it. Whether it's ego or testosterone I'm not sure, but it certainly is more difficult.

I awoke on the morning of 9 August 1998, still inside the prison ward but with a sense of purpose as regards the cancer. Surgery was scheduled for the eleventh and I felt equipped to face the challenge, was even eager for it and for the transition to the next stage of the recovery. Breakfast was a massive treat inside the hospital; you'd often get eggs or pancakes as opposed to the stale bread that was dished up in the prison. The guards hated us enjoying ourselves and it was really the only way I could get back at them; small victories were important ones, though, so I looked forward with relish to breakfast every morning.

This day was to be different, though. By 8 a.m. I was starting to feel a bit nauseous. I had tried to pass urine and a motion at least twice already and nothing was happening. The guards were losing their cool and I knew that there was only so far I could push them. It was National Day, the biggest public holiday of the year in Singapore, marking the day they gained independence from the United Kingdom. There was only a skeleton staff in the hospital. My lucky streak was shining bright again. The nausea continued unabated. I was throwing up and my stomach was starting to become distended. I was receiving injections on the hour for the nausea but had not seen sight of a doctor all day. Two nurses arrived, armed with two tubes and a bucket to perform colonic irrigation in full view of the ward. It was the most painful thing I had ever experienced and I still can't understand to this day why someone would go through this process willingly, and furthermore pay for it! Nothing was working; my stomach now looked as if someone had inserted a medicine ball under the skin and it was slowly making its way towards my chest. Tubes were inserted in my nose to drain off some of the fluid and acids in my stomach. I must have retched at least twenty times when they were inserting them and then, not being able to face the discomfort, promptly removed them. I chanced my luck at going to the toilet once more and felt unmentionably weak as they unlocked the leg chain and I tried to stand. As the guard turned his back to return to the command post, I did my damnedest to make it to the toilet. I reached the toilet bowl and passed out, awaking to a Lilliputian world where everything had increased in size except me. I was man-handled to the bed and eventually taken for an x-ray, where it was revealed that my lung had collapsed. They still thought I was messing about, though, as they shackled me hand and foot in the wheelchair and took me to the x-ray room. The next thing I knew I was on an operating table being prepped to go into theatre. The great and good from the hierarchy of the prison authority were assembled, anxious to see what was going to unfold in the next episode of my life. This unlikely gathering watched on as I was pushed into the operating theatre.

I was to spend another ten days in a mixture of intensive care and the prison ward. A third of my colon had been removed and I had 38 staples in the wound in my stomach and was stuffed with various tubes that were removing blood and an assortment of fluids from my body. On the morning of 20 August, the staples were removed and I was transported back to Tanah Merah Prison. I weighed 65 kilos. I returned the soiled hospital visit uniform and replaced it with the standard-issue navy prison shorts with my number – 38406 – emblazoned on them. My legs disappeared into them and the stark reality of how much weight I had lost finally hit home. I was taken back to B wing and placed in a cell of my own. For three long years I had sought to get a cell on my own, but now I had it I was soon to find out that I couldn't cope.

I tried to lower myself to the floor to get ready for sleep but, however I manoeuvred my body, different sets of pains would shoot up through my stomach. I had no stomach muscles left as they had all been severed during the operation and there was nothing in the trunk of my stomach to steady my movements. With the aid of the small wall that provides some privacy for the inmates when they are going to the toilet, I managed almost to reach the floor but felt myself falling the last two or three inches. Sleep came painfully but the morning would offer a different conundrum – getting up. The lights came on at 7 a.m. as usual, but it was eight before I was in a prone and standing position. The morning muster found me doubled over and holding my stomach; the wound had split. It was patched up later that morning and slowly healed to leave a scar that is an inch in circumference around my belly button.

All of this gave me more to rail about to the prison authorities. I needed a bed to lie on; I needed better food to aid my recovery and, most of all, I needed a doctor who was a little more sympathetic and unlikely to make mistakes, such as telling me it was down to age! My time in the punishment cells served me well. The authorities knew I could be a stubborn so and so when I wanted to be and they knew that I meant what I said now. Rather than driving my anger inside of myself, I was directing all my efforts at the guards and the authorities to achieve what I needed. There were clearly things I couldn't do after the operation – from simple tasks like picking objects up from the floor to more complicated things like exercise. This created a feeling of resentment and anger that needed to be refocused and made to work for me. This wasn't a silly game like I played when I had been in the punishment cell; this was real and involved my health and recovery. My intention wasn't to be as difficult and problematic as I could but I wasn't going to be a sponge any more and simply soak up everything they threw at me.

I was moved to the sick bay to be on my own. There was a metal bed there, minus a mattress, but at least this minor upgrade meant I didn't have to lower myself to the floor every evening. The running water was constant so I could shower when I needed, and the room was larger and airier than the standard cell. Every now and then my sanctuary would be invaded by an inmate who had lost it during the evening and would arrive, handcuffed hand and feet to a similar metal bed, but it wasn't that often. Occasionally it would be someone I knew so I would have someone I could talk to. I was given extra rations of food as well as the luxury of cold baked beans every day. These small victories were important to me and made me feel better about life.

Along with the letters that I was still receiving, the small improvements gave me the momentum that allowed me to move from day to day. Probably for the first time in the history of a Singaporean prison an inmate was offered a course of chemotherapy. I was visited by an eminent oncologist and was told it would increase my chances of beating the illness, although I was warned of some of the side-effects. I was obviously eager to proceed but it wasn't long before there was another obstacle put in the way. There was a chance that I would respond badly to the treatment and would be hospitalised. As far as I was concerned, there was only one way that could happen – without the leg cuffs. When I had been taken into hospital before I didn't know what was going to happen and I had been appalled at being chained to a bed day and night like something from the Middle Ages. The indignity this brought is without equal. I would not knowingly put myself in that situation again. I refused the chemotherapy.

Within hours I was paid a visit by someone from the head of the Prison Service.

'Mr Leeson,' he began, 'we are offering you chemotherapy but I am being told that you are refusing the treatment. You understand the benefits of this course of treatment. Are you crazy?'

'I'm not crazy,' I replied. 'But I will also never knowingly or willingly be leg-cuffed to a bed again in my life.'

He twirled around a piece of paper that he had been casually turning over as we talked so that I could see it.

'It is standard operating procedure,' he said. 'There is nothing that either you or I can do about it.'

'I can. I will not have the chemotherapy, and it's as simple as that. You have an impregnable prison ward yet you still chain people to the bed. If you go to the zoo and see lions and tigers in a cage, they're not chained to the cage. I will not allow you to treat me like a dog,' I ended.

A day or so later I got my wish. I was starting to get a bit of a smile back on my face. After so many things going against me for so many years, things weren't quite as frightening as they had been and I now firmly believed that I would see out the remainder of my sentence and have a future – a future I hadn't been sure existed just a couple of months earlier.

As the days passed and I received my first dose of chemotherapy I had to change my daily routine and pace myself accordingly. Chemotherapy is an especially demanding form of treatment and, while I didn't have any family, work or social commitments that I had to be concerned about, changes needed to be made. I'd feel terrible after the chemo, totally unable to eat and lethargic, but in the mornings I'd have a burst of energy that I just wanted to burn and burn until I exhausted it. I'd run and exercise like a madman, showing the world inside those four walls that I could cope and that I could go from strength to strength. Every now and then one of the officers would walk over to the exercise bars and ask me not to do any more pull-ups as he could see the strain on my stomach. I'd agree and then, as he marched back to the main office, I'd sneak in another two or three, smiling at the security cameras that followed us everywhere. I really felt like I was controlling my own recovery. The chemotherapy was coming into my body and I was forcing it around and through the other side as quickly as possible. I'd eat like a horse at breakfast and lunchtime in the knowledge that in the evening I wouldn't be able to touch so much as a grain of rice.

As the courses passed I drew a lot of support from the nurses who administered the treatment. We had a strange sort of camaraderie that was impossible inside the prison and I was reminded vaguely of my old life back home. It was therapy itself just to have a bit of a laugh and a joke. They used to take great delight in sending me back to Singapore's highest security prison, full of the most dangerous elements of Singaporean society, with Bart Simpson plasters on the areas where the catheter had been inserted.

This camaraderie represented a reality that I alone in the prison owned and I never wanted to let it go. And, rather than being a depressing time, my chemotherapy was something I looked forward to. I still had the handcuffs on when walking to the treatment areas, where they were taken off, but there would be Ince (Mr) Din and Ince (Mr) Chua, both shoulder-high to a grasshopper at about four foot five, weighing in at about 40 kilos a piece, escorting me through the hospital. It must have made for a very amusing sight.

It is important to smile and recognise the ironies of life, but if you've been diagnosed with a serious disease, you can't smile all the time, of course. That's when you need to look for positives, however small, in your daily life and focus on them. Empowering yourself with information and the support you need from friends and family can be an enlightening experience that can enable you to overcome the obstacles.

## IN CONVERSATION

**IVAN**

So then you got cancer …

**NICK**

I did. And it gave me another battle to fight.

**IVAN**

Something else to focus on?

**NICK**

Yes. People sent me material to read. And, because my body was invaded by a dreadful disease that I was totally ignorant of, I devoured it all. So cancer became a strong focus of attention. It coloured every day from that date forward and still does today. Your body is a very important informational tool; nobody knows it better than you so it's important to know what it is telling you. I had to become knowledgeable about it so as to play a major role in the healing process I was about to undertake. That new focus meant that last part of the prison sentence went by very quickly. Many of the inmates and prison warders and officers who knew me did genuinely feel a little sorry for me and the predicament I was in once I was diagnosed with cancer. They expected me to be very, very ill while undergoing chemotherapy in the hospital. But I wasn't going to let that happen. The stubborn streak in me said I wasn't going to give in to the cancer and allow it to destroy me. I wanted to be as well equipped as possible to deal with the chemotherapy. Throughout my period of incarceration, exercise was the dominant theme. It may be a bit of a cliché but a healthy body did lead to a healthy mind. It was probably more important after the operation than before as it was something I could gauge my recovery against; it's still an important tool now. Chemotherapy makes you more susceptible to sunburn but even in a hundred-degree heat I would exercise as hard as I could. I wasn't supposed to go in direct sunlight while having the chemotherapy with all the toxic drugs swimming around inside me but I did in order to exercise. I remember when the drugs were administered they would be housed in a black bag so as not to be affected by the lights in the room. Rather stupidly I didn't afford myself the same sort of protection but I felt so much better sweating and forcing the drugs through my body, rather than passively allowing them to pass through. I felt I was forcing them through, and again that gave me an element of control.

**IVAN**

Did you have an image in your mind of yourself forcing the drugs round your system?

**NICK**

Definitely. The drug wasn't controlling me. I was controlling *it* and having a say in what it was doing. I knew it had to go into my body and round my veins and it had to do what it had to do, but I could get it through me as quickly as possible by exercising. I wasn't just going to sit back and passively allow it to meander through my veins. It would probably still do a good job but it was going to make me feel ill for a longer period. By exercising and sweating I was forcing this drug through me in double-quick time. If I'd just sat back and relaxed and gone with the flow, I'd probably have felt sick.

**IVAN**

Do you talk to cancer experts about that approach?

**NICK**

I do.

**IVAN**

And do they say that that makes scientific sense?

**NICK**

No, they don't, not really. But nobody will change my mind about it. If I had had chemotherapy early in the morning I would have had to wipe out all of those days and would have been moping around. Not being able to do anything about it would have pushed me to the brink of depression.

**IVAN**

So it makes psychological sense.

**NICK**

Oh definitely. I think there is some scientific basis for it. But it's not something they necessarily look into. For a couple of days, when I was first had chemotherapy, I was given the drugs in the morning. This wiped out my day because I'd go to the hospital, have chemotherapy at ten o'clock in the morning, go back to the prison and I wouldn't be able to eat food at lunchtime or in the evening. So of course we realised I would suffer severe weight loss if I took the chemotherapy like that. So they changed it to the afternoon and it was so much better because I'd have breakfast and lunch before going over to the hospital to have the chemo. So in the morning I could eat, at lunchtime I could eat, and in between I could exercise. The day wasn't wasted. I really do believe that the timing of when you have chemotherapy can be important because if you have it first thing in the morning your day's gone. It's then difficult to have the motivation to exercise. Obviously one gets periods of nausea when the anti-nausea drugs are not being administered, but that's a small price to pay. They're quite addictive.

Once that routine was established I had a great feeling of success from just getting the chemo through my body in a way that wasn't impacting on my life at the time. When my stomach muscles healed up I could exercise as hard as I used to before. The operation incision was from just above my groin area to just below my chest, a good thirteen-, fourteen-inch cut through my stomach muscles.

I had the emergency operation on the ninth of August and on the twentieth of September they took the staples out. In the afternoon they sent me back to the prison to start lying on the concrete floor again. The wound split open again but nevertheless, within a couple of weeks, I was trying to do stomach exercises, just because I didn't want to give in to the disease. And that was very important for me. I wanted to be well again and achieve what I did before.

I can totally understand when people who get cancer have to change their lifestyle, particularly when it happens later in life. They have to make choices, maybe to not do everything they did before, and that can be debilitating. But they *have* to look for other interests, other avenues to get involved in. You don't have to go from having four interests to having one when you have cancer. You can maintain that one and find another three to incorporate into your new lifestyle that will give you enjoyment and a sense of wholeness. Then you don't feel the disease has taken everything from you. I didn't want to give anything away. I wanted to keep it all.

**IVAN**

A lot of people, when they have an illness, think that they *are* the illness, that it is part of them. It's a fundamental psychotherapeutic principle that such people need to separate their core identity from their illness. I'm very impressed that you worked this out for yourself. You weren't the cancer. It was just another problem you had to work at. This is in marked contrast to those people who psychologically collapse when they get a serious illness because they internalise it, so that the illness becomes part of their identity. The same applies to someone who comes to believe that they are an 'addict' or an 'alcoholic' or a 'depressive': they cannot use their inner resources against the problem. Therapeutically it has a huge impact on people when you help them realise they are not the problem. In effect, you stumbled on the best survival strategy possible.

## STRESS AND THE IMMUNE SYSTEM

It would come as no surprise to health scientists that Nick Leeson developed cancer in prison. The chance of falling ill after experiencing a prolonged period of stressful setbacks, which have prevented innate needs from being met, is well understood and known to be high. Research published in the *Journal of the American Medical Association*, for example, found that people without friends, whose need for connection to the wider community was not being met, were *four times* as likely to come down with cold symptoms after intentional exposure to a cold virus than people with a wide variety of close friends. Major diseases such as cancer have been similarly linked to the stress of emotional needs not being met.

Chemical messengers called peptides flow around the bloodstream mediating emotional responses between the brain and the body. Many of these, such as endorphins, are directly associated with emotions and each of your immune cells have receptors for all of these chemical messengers, as does your gut and most other internal organs. They are in two-way communication with your brain, particularly your limbic system, where 85–95 per cent of the receptors are concentrated and from where your deep emotions and instinctive drives arise.

When we stretch ourselves and successfully achieve a goal, nature, via these peptides, gives us feelings of pleasure and well-being *and strengthens the immune system.* This is nature's reward system for when we make an effort to learn and adapt and it indicates that we are thriving and our immune system responds by working at peak efficiency so that you can survive and reproduce. The feeling of exultation that follows successfully dealing with a challenge actually energises your immune system. So, when you deal well with a stressful challenge and satisfy your need for control over events, it actually helps you maintain good health.

And the opposite is true. Feeling hopeless in the face of stressful situations that we perceive as insurmountable destroys good health. Just as animals separated from the herd often quickly die from disease, humans who feel chronic hopelessness are extremely vulnerable to disease, including cancer. In short, the human immune system is significantly weakened by helpless reactions to stress and strengthened by stress that is dealt with successfully.

An example of experimental proof of this comes from research into an important part of the body's immune system: the natural killer cells. These amazing fighting units have the ability to recognise and selectively kill both cancer cells and virus-infected cells. Experimenters have actually measured variations in natural killer cell activity based on interactions between stress and attitude. For example, Dr Steven Locke at Harvard Medical School questioned subjects about stressful events in their life and also about their psychiatric symptoms of distress. He then took blood samples and used them to measure their natural killer cell activity. The subjects were sorted into four equal-sized groups according to the level of their stress and the degree of their symptoms.

The median killer cell activities measured for the four groups were as follows:

| GROUP | NATURAL KILLER CELL ACTIVITY |
|---|---|
| ▸ **Good coping** (high stress/low symptoms) | 22.5 |
| ▸ **Lucky** (low stress/low symptoms) | 15.1 |
| ▸ **Neurotic** (low stress/high symptoms) | 10.6 |
| ▸ **Bad coping** (high stress/high symptoms) | 7.5 |

The killer cell activity level of the group with high stress and low symptoms was three times higher than those with high stress and high symptoms. People under severe pressure, who stretch themselves to deal with it, thus appear to have more immune activity than even unstressed people with poor mental habits. Thus nature rewards those who make efforts to survive.

## CANCER PREVENTION AND LIFE REVIVAL

By Dr Rosy Daniel BSc MBBCh – Integrated Medicine
Consultant and former Medical Director of the Bristol
Cancer Help Centre, UK

My introduction to Nick Leeson evolved out of his charity work for the Irish Cancer Help Centre, known as Slanu in County Galway. During 2004 Slanu director Eileen Joyce picked up on my work specialising in reaching those newly diagnosed with the disease. After fifteen years as a doctor and then Medical Director of the Bristol Cancer Help Centre, my first imperative on leaving in 1999 was to create access for all to the model of empowerment and self-healing which had been developed at Bristol over the previous twenty years and is designed to help those with a cancer diagnosis get themselves into the winning statistics. Described by leading UK oncologist Professor Karol Sikora as 'the gold standard in innovative cancer care', this approach has been transformational for the thousand or so people who are treated at the centre in Bristol each year.

However, in the UK alone there are 270,000 new cancer diagnoses yearly and a further million people living with the disease. I was determined that the approach should be available to anyone who needed it. Hence the Cancer Lifeline Kit evolved. The Kit, produced by my new organisation, Health Creation, is designed to catalyse really healthy and fulfilling lifestyle changes to prevent cancer recurrence long term. Nick very kindly described it as the best and most useful 'toolbox' of information and empowering self-help processes he had come across since his diagnosis.

On researching my *Cancer Prevention* book in 1999, even I was stunned to discover that cancer is around 81.5 per cent lifestyle related.

**What I discovered is that in developed countries the cause of cancer is:**
- 35% food – (due mainly to excess consumption of meat, animal fats, lack of fruit and vegetables and high levels of obesity)
- 30% smoking
- 10% excess female hormones from HRT and the pill
- 5% excess alcohol
- 1.5% lack of exercise

**Total 81.5% which is completely under our control, and then:**
- 10% infections (such as Human Papilloma Virus causing cervical cancer)
- 4% electro magnetic radiation (including UV sunlight, radiation, electrical installations, mobile phones and phone masts)
- 4% occupational hazards and pollution
- 0.5% medical procedures (mainly radiation and toxic drugs)

**Many of these factors can be under our control too.**

My success in treating those with cancer has been based on the holistic approach to health – which has as its primary tenet the proposition that the state of our health is a result of the interacting influences of body, mind, spirit and the environment in which we live. So, while many of the factors listed above are physical, the real reasons why people smoke, overeat, drink too much or fail to exercise are always psychological – related to stress, unhappiness, money or relationship problems: the factors covered in this book. Deeper than this is also the fact that, if an individual has lost their way in life, having their spirit crushed or broken, they are in a continual low level (or acute) depression which can have a disastrous effect on their immunity and ability to resist disease.

The key in catalysing a health revival in my clients is almost always to catalyse a 'life revival' – empowering them to embrace life again, to become the person they were always meant to be, free of the 'oughts', 'shoulds' and limiting beliefs and behaviours which have crushed their spirit and taken away the pleasure in life. But, of course, to make a radical difference to the incidence of cancer and heart disease (which is caused by all the same things) is a really tall order. Most of us know full well the things we do that are damaging us but we go on in the same patterns for years – becoming an 'accident waiting to happen'. The reason we do this is because we are never shown clearly the ways in which we are making ourselves vulnerable and neither do we receive the absolutely vital encouragement, guidance and support to change our health-defining behaviour. It is clear to me that these do not change through information alone – if so, no one could sit with a message saying smoking kills in front of them and still smoke. We need to change our underlying states of mind, beliefs and energy levels to give up our bad habits and replace them with positive ones that can give us the same comfort or buzz without harming us.

Part of my Health Creation Programme includes a self-assessment tool called 'The Picture of Health' – which enables you to analyse specific areas in your life as having strengths and weaknesses.

## The Picture of Health before completion

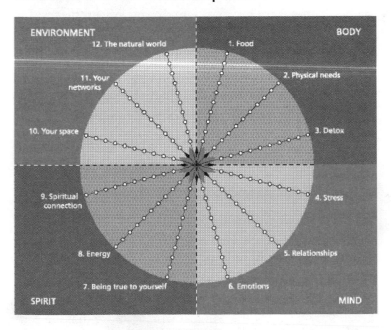

The Picture of Health is based upon 12 Health Creation Principles – 3 for body, 3 for mind, 3 for spirit and 3 for environment. Each of the principles is represented as a 'spoke' on the pictogram above and is scored from 0 to 10 *from the centre outwards.*

All you have to do is to answer 10 questions for each principle 'yes' or 'no' and plot your score on to the relevant principle. When you have completed all twelve, you then join up the dots and shade in the central area created. This is a real eye-opener, because immediately you can see the central area, which represents the part of you, which is strong, and the outer remaining areas in each quadrant where you may be at risk. The full Picture of Health kit is comprised of 120 questions (details of how to order the kit are at the back of the book) but here are two sample sets of questions. Try them out and see where you score on the diagram:

**PRINCIPLE 1 – RELATING TO 'FOOD':**

1 Do you eat a diet that is high in fresh fruit and vegetables (eating fresh fruit and vegetables at every meal)?

2 Do you eat plenty of your fruit and vegetables raw as salads or juices?

3 Do you buy vegetables that are locally grown, fresh and organic?

4 Do you avoid eating saturated animal fats (from butter, cheese, milk, yoghurt, eggs, meat, bacon, sausages, salamis, meat pies, ice-cream and fried foods)?

5 Do you avoid eating a diet that is high in animal protein from meat, fish, eggs and cheese?

6 Do you eat a diet that is mainly 'brown' and unprocessed (eating brown bread, flour, whole-wheat pasta and brown rice)?

7 Do you avid using a lot of added salt in your diet?

8 Do you avoid eating a lot of sugar in hot drinks, cold drinks, sweets, desserts, cakes and pastries?

9 Do you avoid buying sweets, crisp and sweetened drinks that are high in calories and low in nutritional value?

10 Do you avoid food and drinks that contain stimulants such as tea, coffee and caffeine drinks?

**PRINCIPLE 4 – RELATING TO STRESS:**

1 Do you feel free from continual fear and insecurity?

2 Do you feel free from anxiety about what you have to achieve or about your performance at home or at work?

3 Are you able to cope with your life without needing excessive drink, drugs, gambling, emotional reassurance or sex to help you cope with your anxiety?

4 Are you able to stop working within normal working hours (or do you feel the need to continue working all possible hours)?

5 Are you able to do a 'good enough' job instead of continuously striving for perfection?

6 Are you content to work at a steady pace rather than pushing yourself?

7 Do you work to satisfy your own standards (or are you constantly striving to win the approval of others)?

8 Do you balance work time with rest, play or recreational time?

9   Do you set yourself realistic achievable goals that are well within your capacity in terms of time, energy and money?

10  Are you free of the symptoms of stress such as a racing heart, palpitations, trembling hands, excessive sweating, muscular tension and a racing mind that will not stop even when you do?

Ask yourself these questions now and count up your number of yes answers. If you have scored five or less on either I would recommend that it is time to get cracking with improving your own health.

On the opposite page is an example of a completed Picture of Health done by a high-powered businessman in a position like Nick was in at Barings Bank. What is immediately obvious is that while he highly self-expressed (principle 7) and thinks he is protecting himself by staying really fit (principle 2) he is actually at great risk because he is highly stressed (principle 4), with very low energy levels (principle 7), an appalling over-rich diet (principle 1) and with very little protective love in his life (principle 5). He also has a poor relationship with his community and the environment and is missing out here too on the protection of a sense of belonging locally and making a contribution to society. I call this picture 'the heart attack special' because he has all the key risks of stress, over-rich diet and lack of love, intimacy and a sense of belonging to his community which are the major predictors of coronary artery disease, heart attacks and strokes.

## The Picture of Health chart of a high-achieving businessman

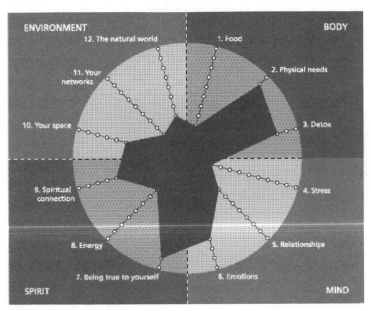

Once this man saw his chart and understood the holistic health model and science behind it, he committed himself to change. We started by giving him energy support with acupuncture, as he was too drained to contemplate change without first receiving some energy input. He then chose to have massage and learn relaxation to lower his tension levels. After three months' regular mentoring, we analysed his stress. Once his energy levels were higher, he then felt able to plan some changes at work, to relieve his stress and free up some time so that he could switch more focus into his marriage. At the four-month point he decided to drop his aggressive gym routine for a combination of cycling and yoga, which he found far more calming and energising. The final change in months five and six was to get his diet on a healthy footing. He says, 'Now I've seen there is no going back, and my recovery starts with the love I feel for my life and my family, and the time with them is non-negotiable.'

Needless to say, his life became richer and better by the day and he feels he still achieves just as much at work because he arrives in a much better frame of mind. His blood pressure has dropped from 150/100 to 130/85 and his weight has dropped by a stone, too. Once you embark upon a Health Creation Programme you will be supported to address your own patterns and blind spots and make your own action plan for healthy change. At the heart of this will be a great deal of support and care to ensure that the root cause of any distress or wound, which is causing you not to care for yourself properly, is addressed. You will also look at what or who is currently dominating your life and keeping you stuck. Ultimately you will be supported to swap that in life which drains, inhibits or damages you for that which enlivens, energises and turns you on, being supported to heal the past as you go through the programme.

> ► **REMEMBER:** Happy excited people have happy excited immune systems and bodies that can resist disease.

Nick Leeson was able to turn his life around once he was able to take a good look at the factors that had made him ill. He has a brighter future now than he has had for many years. Although he never says he is *cured* of cancer, he has a much better idea of how stress and an impoverished, if high-status, lifestyle can eat away at the quality of the precious thing that is life.

# chapter 7
## MONEY WORRIES –
# living with debt and the credit-card culture

**NICK'S STORY**

Most parents will try to shield their kids from any serious money worries they may have. With two stepchildren and a newborn of my own I know this most definitely to be the case. We provide the toys, the latest clothes and the ubiquitous holidays abroad without showing any sign to them that it's often a struggle. When I was growing up, there wasn't always enough work for my mother or father to remain employed and often was the time when we struggled as a family to make ends meet. More often than not my mother and father would bear the brunt of the shortfall and go without stuff for themselves so that we kids could have new clothes and toys. Some of my earliest memories, interspersed with the many happy ones, recall periods when there were definitely money problems in the house.

For a while we had one of those old televisions with a meter attached that was on a timer. You had to put fifty pence in the meter every day or so, and at the end of the week a man would come around and collect the cash. My brother and sisters remained oblivious to what was happening, but there were times as I got older that I noticed the fifty-pence pieces would be recycled through the system, passing through two, three and sometimes four times so that we could watch the TV. It was false economy at its rawest level, as the day was always dawning when the telly man, as he was known, would come round asking for his money. All the phantom fifty pences would have to be accounted for and tally with the usage. I bet Barings would have liked some of those simple, infallible checks that are impossible to subvert. They never quite got round to it.

If things were particularly bad, when Saturday came around we'd all be hiding in the kitchen, staying silent until the telly man had been and we'd gained another week's grace in making up the shortfall. This is probably my first experience of a stressful situation; my mother was always a little bit more difficult to deal with on these days, her tension apparent in the way we were brusquely dealt with. The normal, caring parent–child relationship was usurped by the stress she was feeling. Not until she had gained that grace of another week would she return to normal. I don't think anyone has metered TV or a telly man these days but, despite the sophistication of modern living, I don't think the way many of us manage our finances has changed that much. Postponement, whether it be of credit-card repayments or refinancing through new or consolidation loans very much seems to be the order of the day. The similarities between this and my own calamitous behaviour at Barings is frightening – robbing Peter to pay Paul. Postponing the realisation of the losses or the credit-card repayments until they are impossible to repay is a recipe for ruin.

As Dickens's Micawber calculated before being carted off to debtor's prison: 'Annual income twenty pounds, annual expenditure nineteen, nineteen six, result happiness. Annual income twenty pounds, annual expenditure twenty pounds ought and six, result misery.' Many of us are fast-tracking that misery; emboldened by low interest rates and easy access to credit. We now readily accept living it up on borrowed cash as a way of life. I was no different; to a degree that was the way I used to live. I have a different set of circumstances now, though; nobody would dare lend me money any more. Or so you would think. No sooner had I stepped off the plane, back in England after four and a half years in jail for the biggest financial scandal of the decade, if not the century, than I was inundated with offers for credit cards, loans and an astonishing array of credit facilities. The liquidators had just served me with an injunction for £100 million. The story of that and of the 'rogue trader' returning home were splashed across the front pages of the newspapers and yet I was being offered credit by pretty much every bank you can name.

The first letter that hit the doormat after my return home, rather than a welcome home letter, was a credit-card application. How had I managed to do this? What piece of skulduggery had I managed to pull off this time? Simple: I was back on the electoral roll. I was receiving preferred applications for gold and platinum cards all because I was a name again on an electoral register. Absurd, isn't it? A hundred million pounds in debt, no job, not much likelihood of a job, a proportion of my earnings assigned to the liquidators and yet here were banks offering me credit. I ask you, when did they expect to get repaid? After the first £100 million it would have all been plain sailing.

That's how easy credit is to get. I have none in the eyes of the world's financial markets but they'd all like to give me some in another respect. During some of the meetings that the House of Commons Treasury select committee held this year, it was discovered that a bank had sent an application form for a gold card with a £10,000 credit limit to a dog called Monty. Now I don't know Monty personally, but he still probably represents a better credit risk than yours truly.

The financial services industry is principally to blame for creating this credit culture that leaps out at us from pop-ups on computer web pages or is splashed all over our television screens in the form of adverts fronted by slick-looking salespeople and emblazoned on billboards as we go about our daily business. The task force that was set up by the government in October 2000 to tackle the problem of over-indebtedness reported an 'overt trend in marketing towards the ease, speed and scale of credit availability, and offering incentives and inducements to borrow'. Clearly this presents a misleading picture of easy money that we've all been pulled towards over the years and runs counter to the message that borrowing needs to be thought about, earned and repaid. If you don't think carefully about it, if you don't earn it and repay it, it's very quickly going to become stressful. If not managed correctly it may prompt you to take chances, much as I did in Singapore, with money lenders charging extortionate rates to keep your head above water.

Has the government done anything to curb this form of advertising as they have with smoking or alcohol? The

answer is no. Much of the credit-related advertising has simply replaced those formerly emblazoned with tobacco spon-
sorship on your favourite football team's jerseys or as
advertising on Formula One racing cars. Non-cardholders
are being bombarded by direct mail solicitations, offering
interest-free deals on balance transfers and new purchases,
loyalty schemes and even free gifts. For a compulsive shop-
per existing in a debt-loving society, the credit card has
become an irreplaceable tool.

Credit cards remain one of the most expensive forms of
borrowing you could possibly undertake, but more often
than not we are lured by the offer of balance transfers at
reduced or no interest rate. A shrewd move if you are able to
manage your finances correctly, and refrain from taking on
any more debt, but that is rarely the case. More often than
not the reason someone is transferring their balance is
because they have had some difficulty keeping up the repayments. You are then left with two credit cards, increased
capacity to spend, with no subsequent increase in your ability to manage your finances correctly. Several months down
the line many people find themselves looking for a third
credit card to transfer the balance to, usually find it and the
cycle begins again.

Fuelled by the pressures of our consumer-driven society
it's very difficult to see where the limits are. How many credit
cards can you have? If you have more than one, there could
be a problem. Look at it logically, based on your circumstances and ability to repay: one credit card company is willing to lend you a figure of X. Why then would a second credit
card company offer you a credit limit of an amount equal to
or greater than X without an improvement in your personal

circumstances? The control procedures really aren't that good; you can invent yourself a title, a salary or even a new persona. Credit cards remain the fastest-growing credit product with gross advances in this category dominating the total market.

I see a striking similarity here to the way I was behaving during my time in Singapore at Barings. As long as head office were sending me money I would use it, doubling down, increasing my position and exposure while postponing the realisation of the losses. As long as they sent me the money I could use it and stretch, often by my fingertips, into another month. Each and every time they sent the money the positions would increase and the stress would be ratcheted up to the next level. Barings had the doors closed on them by Barclays, Citibank and the rest of the money markets and were unable to borrow any more money to send me in Singapore. It was only then that the realisation dawned on them that something was amiss.

A similar disservice is being provided to all of us by these easy credit facilities. The risk here is very personal. Unsecured personal loans – balances outstanding – continue to grow and dominate the credit product market. Worryingly, though, the growth of new business in this category has experienced a slowdown in recent times as a result of competition from secured loans, suggesting that this credit product has already reached its peak. Negative equity and record personal bankruptcies in the aftermath of the late 1980s boom calmed the appetite for debt but, in the last few years, households have been building up debt at increasing rates. Even more worryingly more and more people are remortgaging their properties to release equity now and, rather than looking forward to a lazy retirement on the beach, they are going to be working longer to repay the loans that they have outstanding.

As of the beginning of 2005, a study found that more than half of all personal bankrupts are now under thirty. The number of declared insolvents has passed the 50,000 mark – an all-time record and a 65 per cent increase on those of a decade ago. Whereas in the past bankruptcy was usually triggered by a major life crisis such as illness, divorce or death of a spouse, today's bankrupts are often in full-time jobs but have crippled themselves by living above their means to an excessive degree. With this study freshly published, news broke of a new credit card specifically aimed at low-income families becoming available. The card – known as Vanquis – sets a typical interest rate of 49 per cent but high-risk borrowers could face interest of up to 70 per cent. The card has been designed to target people with an annual income of half the national average.

With 67 million credit cards in circulation in the UK, Britain holds more than the whole of the rest of Western Europe combined. Our addiction to credit is fuelling the boom of borrowing but, in the long term, this behaviour will inevitably lead to thousands of cases of personal disaster – caused by the stress of insolvency and, in increasing numbers of cases, even the suicide of people unable to cope with what – in a moment's weakness – seems like a 'good idea at the time'.

As a percentage of a bank's overall lending portfolio, the individual accountholder represents such a minuscule percentage that the bank can pretty much discount you as a risk. Only in the event of wholesale defaulting on credit balances or loans would the lender really take much interest. They have very limited risk – the ideal scenario for them, as the individual assumes it all. By not maintaining repayments on any of the credit instruments you hold, you are assuming major risk implications on your possessions: your household, your livelihood, your life. The stress this manifests in your life is often overpowering. For the first time since 1996, real incomes have been falling as a result of increased costs and taxes by stealth, higher and only modest increases in salary, but this still does little to deter the hungry consumer. Britons have continued to pile on debt at a record pace in order to fund a house-price and consumer-spending boom, despite the subdued global economy. The consumer is clearly keeping the economy afloat, but it's all being done on tick. Obviously being heavily exposed to debt is less dangerous when base rates are 4 per cent than when they are 15 per cent, but a lot of people have overcompensated for these low rates and are living with a 'pay later' mindset towards money management.

Clearly mortgage arrears and home repossessions are running at historically low levels but, even if interest rates were to stay at the levels they are as of early 2005, there will come a point for all of us when we will reach the debt saturation point. Long before we hit that saturation point we will have placed ourselves, our bodies and our families under very damaging levels of stress. This can all be avoided. Lifestyle on credit has fast become a way of life and we are all too easily lured by the increased accessibility.

The banks aren't overly concerned, and neither is the government. The Bank of England may issue a word of caution every now and again but the official view is that higher levels of debt are not just affordable but entirely rational in an environment where interest rates are low. Much as the Singapore Monetary Exchange and the world's financial markets were protected from the collapse of Barings, the banks and the government are similarly protected from your misfortune. In short, they don't really care from a micro-perspective. Should there be a debt crisis, it will be the poorest and the most vulnerable who will suffer. The overall figures for debt exposure disguise the fact that those on low incomes are the most heavily exposed and by far the least able to cope. This is hardly surprising given that Britain's culture of low wages and in-your-face advertising results in excessive borrowing among those who really can't afford it. Barclays CEO, Matt Barrett, famously remarked to the House of Commons Treasury Select Committee that he advised his own children against borrowing on Barclaycard because it was 'too expensive'. We should all take note.

The recent government white paper urges the financial services industry to operate a practice of 'responsible lending'. I question how responsible it can be if so many of the principal lenders feel obliged to offer *me* credit facilities. The recent report of the Turner Commission warned that 12 million Britons are failing to save enough for their old age. Combined with the fact that we are borrowing more and more, the outlook is very gloomy. The country represents a modern-day *Titanic* sailing towards the debt mountain, unable to alter course and weighed down by pensions that underperform and by a government that fails to react. Government ministers are constantly encouraging workers to plug the £27 billion savings gap – the difference between what we are managing to squirrel away and what we should be saving to ensure a comfortable old age. Do so and the use of complex means-tested benefits by the current chancellor may result in you being penalised. Research from Mercer Human Resource Consulting has found that a twenty-year-old Briton would have to save at least £280 a month for their entire working life to escape the disincentive of means-testing altogether. Obviously, to get there, you are going to be considerably worse off while you are of working age. Faith in the private pensions industry has taken a severe knock in the past few years

I'm left thinking of the scene in Monty Python's *Meaning of Life* where the offer to an already obscenely engorged customer of one more 'wafer-thin mint' makes him explode. The offer of one more piece of credit should have the same effect on all of us. Or, as with nicotine products, should come with a very obvious health warning.

## WHAT IS OVERINDEBTEDNESS?

Britons have borrowed record amounts in recent months with research from the Financial Services Authority suggesting that over 6 million households now face moderate difficulties paying their current credit and other commitments.

There is no generally accepted definition of overindebtedness in economic literature. Generally speaking, this term refers to a situation where a household is unable to repay consumer credit or mortgage debts. A survey commissioned for the Task Force on Overindebtedness identified that a high risk of getting into financial difficulties was associated with:

- having four or more current credit commitments
  (i.e. outstanding consumer borrowing, not including
  mortgages)
- spending more than 25 per cent of gross income
  on repayment of consumer credit; or
- spending more than 50 per cent of gross income
  on repayment of consumer credit and mortgages.

Research published in 2003 suggested that at least 7 per cent of UK households were in one or more of these categories.

Surprisingly, recent research has suggested that the problem is now common across all age groups, with retirees, professionals and students alike catching the borrowing bug. A recent survey by Prudential, for example, found that people aged 65 and over now have combined debts of more than £1.1 billion largely as result of the remortgaging craze.

## WHY SHOULD WE WORRY?

The growth in consumer credit has been increasing at a quicker pace than the growth of average earnings since 2001 and, while the disparity in the pace of growth is relatively slight, the trend looks to be on the increase. This is clearly unsustainable in the long term.

Recent figures from the Credit Services Association revealed that the level of arrears being passed to debt-collection firms has soared 70 per cent since 2001, highlighting the increasing difficulties British households experience with repaying their debts.

The UK's Consumer Advice Bureau is now dealing with over a million new debt enquiries per year. Consumer credit enquiries, in particular, have risen by over 55 per cent since 1997–8. The last significant increase in CAB debt enquiries took place during the early 1990s and was the direct result of a deep economic recession.

### Warning signs

One of the main triggers for debt problems is a change in circumstances, involving loss of income, a period of ill health or a relationship breakdown.

For a proportion of clients the level of their commitments relative to their income is such that a relatively small decrease (around 10 per cent) in annual income could turn what were previously manageable payments into debt problems.

Payment Protection Insurance, which might be expected to protect people from the effects of unexpected changes in circumstances, does not help to resolve many of the problems, because the changes are often outside the scope of such insurance policies.

In nearly half the cases, those in debt try to get out of difficulty by borrowing more money.

# IN CONVERSATION

## IVAN

Generally people don't have stress problems unless they feel aspects of their life are out of control. When people become anxious and depressed and end up in therapy it's usually from worrying about one or more of the following things: relationships or a lack of them, health problems, having been traumatised, addiction behaviour, work problems or money worries – losing control over their finances. Obviously most people do not get stressed by losing hundreds of millions of pounds like you did. Is money still a major stressor for you?

## NICK

Sure, I have money worries as I think much of the population of the UK has. My earning potential is extremely haphazard. At times it can be fantastic and I can start to plan ahead but there are other times when I am waiting for the phone to ring and it frustrates the life out of me. Not having a 'proper' job exacerbates all of my money worries. Like a lot of people my first worry is about putting food on the table and thereafter providing for my family. That may sound a little overdramatic but it's not. Most people would look at their career status and probably have a three- or five-year plan as to what they want to do and where they want to do it. As much as I would like to, I can't do that; it's very difficult to look more than a handful of months into the future. I think money worries are rapidly increasing as a cause of stress. If they aren't currently the number-one cause of stress, I doubt whether it will be too long before they are. There's a general unease among people about whether they're going to be able to continue paying the mortgage and their credit-card payments. That's even before they start to think about how they are going to live in their retirement years. Who knows if one's private pension scheme will perform well enough to keep us sufficiently provided for in twenty or thirty years' time. The amount of debt people are in now is enormous; it's totally unrealistic and potentially very dangerous. It can only be sustained if the economy continues to grow. I have money worries like everybody else. I don't really know where my money's going to come from over the next few years. I have a mortgage and loans that need to be repaid. That is clearly not an ideal situation. Credit has become increasingly easy to obtain and I think in the UK we've reached a bubble-bursting situation which is going to blow up in everybody's face fairly soon. The level of debt that a household can undertake has to be monitored more efficiently and controlled far better than it is at the moment. I'm sure that there are people whose level of debt would mirror that of many third world countries. It's never going to be repaid! As lenders are willing to offer credit, it's grabbed with both hands until it spirals out of control, until more often than not the more unscrupulous money lenders remain the only option. There was a court case at the close of 2004 whereby a £6,000 loan with charges and interest repayments got well in excess of £300,000. The lender sought possession of the house but thankfully the judge saw reason.

**IVAN**

Are there really no controls? Is the government not doing anything to make it better?

**NICK**

It is that bad. The fact that I get offered substantial credit suggests that there are no controls. The only controls are personal. We all assume the risk personally but the majority of us have never really received any form of education in managing our finances. A government white paper on responsible lending may assuage a few members of parliament but it does little to help the people on street level who are born into a credit culture and know little else. I can only see it getting a lot worse before it gets any better. At least until the education improves. When I came back from Singapore I was shocked by the rise in the number of pawnbrokers, cheque-cashing establishments and bailiffs. I thought those had died away after the last big property crash in the early 90s, but it seems to be resurfacing. Where do we go next? Debtors' prisons that characterised the eighteenth and nineteenth centuries? Surely not! I would never suggest I was good with money. I don't think anybody would after what I did to Barings. I'm one of those people who tend to spend everything they have. I've never really saved anything, not until recently. My career future has never been more uncertain, so when do I have the opportunity to save, to counteract some of that uncertainty? Talking to you makes me think about my mum and the way she was with money, and subsequently how I am. She would borrow to give us the things we needed and send us on school trips. It wasn't necessarily easy credit, but she always found it. I'm not sure if she used moneylenders or whether it was banks. Not quite the culture that we have now, but I can see the start of my own ambivalence about credit dating back to those times. To a degree, I think we all learn rudimentary financial skills from our parents. I've had to change that since my return from Singapore; be more rational about my finances, more realistic and save in order to buy certain things.

**IVAN**

But when you started at Barings they thought you were good with money. Because you were, up to a point.

**NICK**

Yeah, I was. I could calculate quickly and I was extremely accurate, all good attributes when you work in a bank. But it wasn't my money; it was more of a mathematical aptitude test than managing one's own finances. There's a big difference between playing with other people's money and looking after your own. Your own money is more meaningful. When you're dealing in millions of pounds every day it loses its value. As I said, I can see that some of my attitude towards money was shaped by my mum in those early years. She would borrow to get what she wanted, even if she ended up borrowing from one person to pay another.

**IVAN**

But she was around at the time hire purchase boomed and credit cards were introduced. My parents were born in the earlier part of the last century and were brought up never to borrow money. They would only buy what they had saved for and could afford. But that philosophy has gone.

## NICK

Now everything's loans and credit cards. The message is that, if you want something, you should have it now. Buy now, pay later. The message is screamed at you from every advertising hoarding, every magazine or paper. You really can't avoid it. Controlled credit is fine, but a lot of people are leveraging their debt far too highly and very quickly have trouble keeping up the repayments. Stress is the natural consequence, but unfortunately, with money worries, this can often manifest itself in far more damaging ways such as suicide.

## IVAN

And that philosophy undermines a fundamental stage people need to go through to mature properly: that of learning to delay gratification. Research shows that, if children of about four or five years can delay gratification, they are the ones who are going to do well in life, academically, in relationships and in their careers. And the ones that don't learn that lesson will have the most problems in life.

## NICK

The more unfortunate parts of my life story, the collapse of the bank and everything I have experienced thereafter have really cemented that for me. Mackensey has a very important lesson coming to him shortly after his fourth birthday. Maybe he will be the Governor of the Bank of England after all.

## IVAN

The first credit card to be introduced in this country was called Access. And, once it was introduced, everything changed. I remember the advertising slogan they used to launch it: 'Take the waiting out of wanting.' If you think about what that really means – it's a psychopath's charter. Out went the idea that you had to wait and plan and save and work hard if you wanted something.

## NICK

Who picks up the debt when people die? Debt has to go somewhere, whether a bank takes a lien on people's estates when they pass away or their children are sold into slavery to pay off their parents' debts – as still happens in parts of India and Africa. I'm sure we're going to end up with a situation where people die with nothing to pass on except debt. Credit is far too easily available. I owe the liquidators £100 million and yet I get people offering me credit cards all the time! When do they expect to get paid? After I've paid back the £100 million? It's nonsensical. There's supposed to be responsible lending these days in the UK but it's anything but. There are stories about people having their home repossessed and the day before it's supposed to happen they get an offer letter from the same bank offering them a loan. How can that happen? The banking culture is making so much money and is so well capitalised that it can withstand a bit of debt and have a little consideration for the individual circumstances of each debt, and the lives it ruins. All bank directors seem to concern themselves with is making money and paying themselves huge bonuses. I'm not sure that there is such a thing as ethical banking; they sell or offer loans as easily as a salesman would try to sell double glazing or conservatories. They have no interest in whether you need it or can afford it; they are just looking at the bottom line and how much money they are making.

## IVAN

The western way of using money and exploiting capital has penetrated all parts of the world now, hasn't it? Even China.

## NICK

Yes, the whole world is moving towards a more selfish individualism. Rather than having a community approach to welfare, where people are more responsible about money and lending is done responsibly, we're getting to the other extreme where individual and whole countries get themselves into severe levels of debt, with very little chance of getting out of it. And the governments and banks are not doing much about it. They're giving out *more* debt. Credit cards should be renamed debt cards. The Internet has also opened up new areas where you can get credit cards and loans. You can acquire a credit card from your favourite football club and a loan from the supermarket as you do your shopping. The wholesale deregulation of this part of the finance industry is the main contributor to the debt mountain. The epitome of all of this is credit cards with zero per cent credit transfers from one card to another. You can build up a balance on one card, possibly have trouble repaying it, apply for a different card, transfer the balance and start all over again with two cards, rather than one. Twice the trouble! The latest innovation even offers cash back on balance transfers. The banks are now allowing people to build up a debt on one card and transfer the debt to another card which offers zero per cent interest rate for six months and an increased limit. People exploiting this are known as 'card tarts'. They push their card up to the limit and then transfer the debt to another card. That's the theory. But in no time most people have several cards pushed up to the limit. It's no different to what I did at Barings. I doubled down all the time. As I lost money, I'd take on a bigger position to keep going in the hope of earning it all back and eventually making a profit. People are doing that with credit cards. When they spend the money they borrow they have, in effect, lost it. It's gone. If you max out on one credit card and transfer debts to another one, hoping that one day you'll win the lottery or something and be able to pay it all back, you are heading for bankruptcy in the long run.

**IVAN**

That's what you did at Barings!

**NICK**

Exactly. And I went to jail for it. You can still go to jail in the UK for not paying off your debts. I don't think there are too many people in jail for that at the moment but, the way the level of debt is rising, society might actually need to create debtors' prisons to deter people from putting themselves into unmanageable situations.

**IVAN**

In a way, because we have created such a consumerist, materialistic culture and actively encouraged people to take out debts, people would feel it was very unfair to suddenly put them in prison for it.

**NICK**

There is no responsible lending any more. I went into a shop the other day and bought a pair of trainers for sixty quid. The girl at the till said to me, 'Do you want our new credit card so you don't have to pay today?' She was prepared to give me a pair of trainers and send a card to me in the post, with a minus sixty quid opening balance, with no control and very little credit check done.

**IVAN**

Just as there were no controls at Barings.

**NICK**

No controls at all. I think the Barings fiasco is a great analogy of how people are individually running their financial affairs now.

**IVAN**

That's really interesting because, in effect, the whole western world is operating as Barings operated: without proper controls over consumerism. It's a free for all.

**NICK**

Seriously, when you're transferring a balance of debt around different banks to raise more money, that's a mind-blowingly irresponsible measure. Individuals can have lots of credit cards. I mean I don't know *how* many you can have, but all they're doing is building a Robert Maxwell-style house of cards, with several different companies transferring the money around. Imagine the amount of stress it causes some people. Eventually your debt is going to concertina out to six or seven times what you started with. Because there is a finite number of cards you can hold, eventually you'll have nowhere else to go, just as I had nowhere to go with the 88888 account. I kept asking Barings for money; they kept sending it, borrowing it most of the time, but then all of a sudden they couldn't borrow any more. Then it blows up in your face. And that's going to happen to everyone who can't service their debts. Each individual is going to be personally penalised because the banks are not going to pay the debt off. They will go after the individual for it. So you're going to lose your house, your car … all you possess. And that will mean serious stress.

**IVAN**

It does seem like governments and banks and corporations are taking a huge gamble on the economy of the world never having another major recession or oil supplies drying up or major wars or some other catastrophe occurring.

**NICK**

It is a big gamble. Look out for the signals: interest rates rising, property prices faltering or falling, more and more people leveraged very highly in terms of their personal debt versus their income. I think the message is very simple: we have a 'needs versus desires' situation and we all desire everything but we don't need everything.

## IVAN

Unfortunately, many people mistake wants for needs. I have treated millionaires for depression, anxiety, addiction and so forth, so having money doesn't necessarily bring happiness, and research confirms that. A lot of people, when they make enough money, retire and stop stretching themselves and, basically, collapse in on themselves. We all *need* to struggle; we *need* challenges; we *need* to be stretched. And, when we are not, our brains lack focus and lose the sense that life is meaningful. It's the same with obtaining what are, by any relative estimation, luxury goods. You don't really *need* a plasma TV, holidays abroad, a new car or a designer kitchen. You might want them, but if you can have them instantly on credit the essential sense of achievement is lost. You are gratified instantly. And the next day you will want something else. In the UK it seems that, over the past few years, ordinary people have suddenly taken it upon themselves to compete with celebrities, royalty and the very richest strata of society in the world – it's crazy.

## NICK

The whole idea that we should delay gratification, take responsibility, to stretch ourselves, through work or whatever, before being rewarded, needs to be instilled in everybody.

## IVAN

You've come a long way, then?

## NICK

I have learned. I've moved forward slightly! I don't gamble with money that I can't afford to lose. And I would regard investing in the Stock Market as a gamble as well. So I'm sensible in that respect.

## TIPS FOR DEALING WITH DEBT

- ▶ If you have credit card debt that's leveraged to the max, STOP NOW. Start taking responsibility and begin to pay off your debt and make sure you are paying at the lowest interest rates possible.
- ▶ Think of a credit card as a DEBT card and call it that. Each time you use it, the debt gets bigger.
- ▶ Switch to a pay-as-you go DEBIT card. If you need extra cash urgently, arrange an overdraft extension rather than take out a credit card.
- ▶ Learn to weigh up what are unnecessary purchases and what are crucial outgoings: paying your mortgage or rent IS essential; upgrading your mobile phone is NOT.
- ▶ When most of us say we have 'nothing to wear' we usually mean we have nothing new to wear that conforms to the latest fashion – which changes every season. Unless you are in the public eye no one cares THAT much about how fashionable/valuable your wardrobe is.

- ▸ Organise a budget. Tally up how much you are spending on what items and see where you can make reductions. Keep a spreadsheet or simple book-keeping system.
- ▸ Learn to enjoy keeping within budget targets – reward yourself with small treats, not hundreds-of-pound splurges.
- ▸ Don't put yourself in tempting retail areas at weekends. Do something else that doesn't involve spending money but is more holistically rewarding: sports, outdoor activities or meeting friends/going to the movies.
- ▸ Don't be seduced by fancy packaging – it all gets thrown away in the end.
- ▸ Use alternative retail zones like eBay and second-hand shops, especially for items like CDs, DVDs etc.
- ▸ Don't be lured into thinking that a wallet bulging with cards is the sign of a successful person. It is the sign of someone who has been seduced by financial institutions!
- ▸ Read the Citizens Advice Bureau web pages about debt: www.adviceguide.org.uk.

DEALING WITH DEBT ◀

# chapter 8
## ADDICTION –
## compulsions and
## contradictions

### NICK'S STORY

Anything that gives you pleasure can be addictive. Personally
I think that my wife is addicted to cappuccino. As some people crave chocolate, crisps or other foodstuffs, my wife has to
have coffee, every day and fairly often. Not just any coffee,
either; it's important that it's cappuccino, and she even has a
list of places that serve it to her taste. A craving for coffee or
chocolate exists at the mild end of the addiction spectrum; it
won't result in financial difficulties and stealing to feed the
habit, but many addictions at the chronic end of the spectrum, such as drugs, alcoholism and gambling, often do.
This is when tensions begin to appear with partners and relatives, placing a very real strain on relationships. Why, then,
do some people bring so much stress into their lives and put
so much strain on their relationships by embracing rather
than rejecting addictive patterns?

A lot of people are afflicted by a compulsive nature. Not realising it, and not being able to control that compulsion, can lead to full-on addiction, as opposed to a mild dependency. I speak from personal experience here. When I was younger, to me there was no point going out for one or two drinks after work; it would always be nine or ten. I realised fairly early into my adult life that I had problems limiting my alcohol intake, and would rather not go out than succumb to my usual pattern. I've never smoked and I could never live with anyone that smoked; my parents put me off that particular vice for life. Growing up in a house where cigarettes and dirty ashtrays were never further than arm's length away was enough to turn my stomach. I never responded to the peer pressure that most of us feel at some stage during our adolescent years, as I regarded smoking as so abhorrent that there was nothing that would ever make me even try. Prison may have been the ultimate test but, much to my amazement, when I arrived at Tanah Merah Prison I was informed it was a non-smoking jail.

I'd never touched drugs, either. I always wondered if I would be able to control my intake. Would I be sensible? As it turned out my first experiment with drugs was at 32 years of age. Freshly released from prison I spent a couple of months in Bali with some friends and decided that this was the time to try what for so many people my age was commonplace.

You can get pretty much what you want on the island; there's a vibrant party scene and drugs are available wherever you may get the urge, despite the severe penalties. Within the space of a week I had tried ecstasy, cocaine and magic mushrooms. And not the normal amounts that you might expect for a total novice. On the first evening I had eight ecstasy tablets; the second night I was chopping up line after line of cocaine and washing them down with magic mushroom milkshakes. It was a level of narcotic intake that would have pushed a hardened drug user to their natural limit. Bordering on the ridiculous, I was very lucky I didn't die. I was out of control; as soon as my normal level of inhibition had been lowered I was speeding along the freeway to oblivion.

I don't remember much of it, but I certainly remember the despair and emptiness at the end of the week when my friends packed up to go home – back to their regular jobs and lives. The temporary highs had been good but the incessant low was more than I could take, and it drummed on relentlessly. My flight home was booked for a month later; I couldn't wait that long so I just packed a bag and beat a hasty retreat to the airport. I remember standing inside Kuala Lumpur Airport awash with the tropical heat, feeling lost and wondering what I was going to do in flip-flops, shorts and a T-shirt when I got back to the January weather. There is nothing quite so incongruously sad as the returning holidaymaker rolling up at Gatwick sporting colourful beach wear and a sun hat. I had to get myself a plan – not to mention some more suitable urban clothing. I wanted to get back to some form of normality, and that for me lay back home in the UK. I have met many ex-pat Brits who have settled into a lifestyle in the tropics, but after so long spent in the oppressive humidity I felt I needed to reconnect with my roots back in Watford – even though it would most likely be grey, drizzling and cold.

Have I touched drugs since? To be honest I have, once or twice, but not in the last two and a half years, although I can still have problems moderating my alcohol intake. Back in the heady days of Barings, Friday and Saturday nights were always reserved for the winding down of the week with friends and a few drinks. More often than not this would be characterised more by excess than by restraint. The idea that problem drinking is a consequence of the way an individual has learned to drink alcohol really rings true for me. My learning to drink was heavily influenced by the social and cultural context in which the drinking occurred. And I think this rings true for many people in the public eye. For instance, every time a star footballer or celebrity admits to their misdeeds with alcohol in the popular press and puts their faith in the twelve-step programme to salvation, the rhetoric of alcoholism as a 'disease' is reinforced in the public mind. But the broader question of the total amount of harm and suffering caused by the misuse of alcohol is often eclipsed by the sensationalism of such stories, concentrating on bad behaviour and squalid photographs.

In attempting to explain alcohol dependency as a cultural or sociological problem rather than a 'disease', one threatens the theoretical basis for 'disease-based' treatment programmes. But there have to be other means of breaking the habit other than by confession and repentance. Any useful definition of alcoholism must include the notion of 'repeated use leading to harm'. The harm caused by alcohol addiction has been classified by American sociologist Ron Roisen into the '4 Ls': liver, lover, livelihood and law. 'Liver' is shorthand for all physical effects as well as psychological distress. 'Lover' stands for problems of interpersonal relationships. 'Livelihood' refers to the inevitable difficulties one will get into with employment, and 'law' represents the various civil and criminal proceedings which may arise from alcohol misuse.

For me, this is an effective reminder of the horrendous potential decline that could await me if I were to take to the bottle, and I wish I had known of the '4 Ls' mantra when I was working in Singapore. During my time in the Far East my drinking rapidly got worse. As the stress started to escalate I'd drink more to get through the endless dinner parties that I would have to attend to talk about work. More often than not I'd black out in the taxi on the way back to our apartment and wake up not remembering what had happened, initially panicked by the fear that I may have let the cat out of the bag. My recollection of the evening before would be minimal; it was as if the drink had washed the slate of my memory clean. Not that it made things any easier the next day, as I had to face the same people again. I had got myself into such a mess of skulduggery and role-playing that not knowing what we had talked about the night before was actually easier than recalling all the lies I had no doubt told.

If it was a work day, I'd stumble into the office stinking of drink, collapse into my seat on the trading floor, and every now and again burst into a bit of trading activity that would invariably add to the position I already had and ratchet the stress up another notch. I arrived in Singapore weighing about eighty kilos, full of life, active, playing football, boxing and eager for the challenge that lay ahead. As things went wrong and I took on more risk and added to the stress that I was under, I quickly ballooned up to 92 kilos, ditched all the physical activity in my life, massively increased the alcohol intake and looked bloated and ill. With hindsight, the difference is obvious. The pictures of that time tell their own story; on arrival in Singapore I looked fit and healthy; on my departure I was bloated and ravaged by stress and depression.

The worst episode was in December 1994: believing in the profits that I was reporting in Singapore, the management of the bank had arranged a glitzy party in Central Station, New York. No expense was spared, and one hundred and fifty people flew in from around the globe to attend this party to celebrate Barings' success, for which I was principally responsible! I've no idea what it cost but it must have stretched into a six-figure sum. In everyone else's eyes I was the star attraction; in the eyes of the only person that could see the truth, me, I was the biggest fraud ever. I couldn't cope with all the pomp and pageantry; it was a sick, expensive joke. I still couldn't come clean, so I hid myself in a bottle of vodka and drank myself senseless. With a modicum of sense I would have stopped what I was doing, to myself and to the bank, but I couldn't press the panic button that would see the whole sham exposed. That evening, the party started and there was one noticeable absentee who was instead lying, totally incapacitated, on a bed in the hotel on Fifth Avenue. I was going nowhere that night, and if I was pushed it would be back to the bottle and nowhere near Central Station.

We left early in the morning, before anyone else was awake, and slithered our way back to Singapore. The drink clouded my judgement in everything I did but quite how no one else saw the behavioural change in their 'star' employee is beyond me.

These days, I very rarely *need* a drink, as I have nothing to cover up, and I certainly don't drink every day. I would rather go without and wake up the next morning feeling refreshed and eager to greet the day. Groggy and burdened with a hangover is no way to spend the 24 hours following the night before. But, if I'm going out socially, alcohol invariably represents a large part of the evening and I will often drink more than is sensible, although nothing like I did when I was at Barings.

Addiction has diversified over recent years – alcohol and tobacco addictions have been added to with cocaine, sex and exercise, all having twelve-step programmes in place for those afflicted. Shopping, too, can be added to that list, with increasing numbers of people becoming addicted to designer labels and, more dangerously, to the credit culture that is often needed to feed it. It is gambling, however, that has particular relevance to my story – more so than the drinking. Like any form of addiction, it can take over your life and lead to corruptive and criminal behaviour. 'Pathological' or 'compulsive' gambling is characterised by unrealistic optimism on the gambler's part, and chronic gamblers are unable to resist the impulses to chance another go. Sound familiar? It should. Eight-hundred-and-sixty-two-million-pounds' worth of losses with record-breaking trading activity would suggest that I was the most compulsive gambler of all time. I always thought that I would get it back – right up until the end of 1994. I couldn't have been more unrealistic; rumours in the marketplace were foretelling my demise but neither I nor anyone at Barings listened to them. Add to that the fact that compulsive gamblers rarely cut their losses or debts and tend to get deeper and deeper into debt, and the story seems only too familiar. If I had cut that first loss, the total would have been £10,000, a far cry from the £862 million.

I never consciously entered the trading floor in the morning thinking that I would increase my position, take on more risk and get all the money back. Invariably I did, though; robotic in my behaviour, I couldn't leave the markets alone and added continually to the position I held. Compulsive gamblers very quickly preoccupy themselves with the gambling, determined that a big win will repay all their debts or, in my case, losses, and solve their problems. My big win never came; Barings was sold for £1 to ING Group of the Netherlands, and the rest is history.

And yet I'm still compulsive. Nobody in their right mind would let me anywhere near a trading floor, but writing for a gambling magazine I often indulge in some of the forms of gambling I write about. I have on-line betting accounts, spread-betting accounts and have even made binary bets that are a more obscure gaming hybrid. All of these accounts I open see a flurry of activity, fed by some form of initial minor success. My activity in these accounts is unrealistic; you can't back the winner in every horse race or football match, just as you can't always predict the movements in the financial markets. I know that, but my compulsive behaviour gets the better of me and I try to do just that. After a couple of weeks of activity, losses eroding the initial profits and moving in the opposite direction, the accounts lie dormant.

These days the most important rule I follow is never to risk money I can't afford to lose. After the initial sums are deposited, my own predefined limits are set. It never happened at Barings but each of us has to take responsibility for our own actions and put those controls in place to dampen the compulsion. Barings may have sent me as much money as I wanted but often in a gambler's life it is family or friends who bail them out. Being bailed out sounds like a safety net or easy remedy but often it's anything but, and family and friends are often doing more harm than good by clearing up the gambler's mess. I've always shied away from the word gambler because I don't like the connotations it throws up. However, it is only recently, through my involvement in particular gaming activities, that I've seen quite how compulsive I can be, and how much that needs to be controlled. So, yes, I suppose I am a gambler.

I've been known to chase a loss or two in my time, or for that matter 862 million of them. But why do people like me do it? We all say we'll never do it again but inevitably people like me fail to keep that promise. So what have I and the other Hall of Fame of rogue traders got in common with anyone who has chased a loss? Well, we all tried to buy ourselves some time and trade or gamble our way out of trouble. But riding the losses until they turn into gains is the same sort of 'masters of the universe' stuff that got us into trouble in the first place. The lesson that should ring loud and clear to everyone is that risk is a four-letter word. And it is not a safe way to make money and get rich. There is an important difference between risk and uncertainty, and making this distinction is crucial. Some economists argue that risk is something you can calculate. Flip a coin and you know for sure what the chances are of getting heads or tails. It might come up heads once, maybe twice or even three times, but you know it won't keep happening.

You add in some uncertainty and it falls apart. Will someone snatch the coin in mid-air? Will you drop dead before it hits the ground? Similarly, the performance of any share price, commodity or currency is driven by uncertain sources that include political, economic, security, social, competitive, managerial and investment factors. Markets also exhibit trends and memories but dice rolls, coin flips and decks of cards do not. You can add to that investors who follow a trend just because everyone else is doing it. The problem is not just that it's impossible to quantify uncertainty – decision-making is far from rational either.

In a well-known experiment, participants were first asked to choose between an 80 per cent chance of winning $4,000 and a 20 per cent chance of winning nothing versus a 100 per cent guarantee of getting $3,000. Despite the chance of them picking up more with the gamble, they overwhelmingly went for the risk-averse choice of $3,000 cold. The participants were then offered an 80 per cent chance of losing $4,000 with a 20 per cent chance of break-even versus a 100 per cent chance of losing $3,000. This time they wanted to gamble. In other words, the certain loss of $3,000 was so intolerable that they were prepared to risk losing more. The major driving force appears to be loss aversion. It's not so much that people hate uncertainty, but rather that they hate losing. This has been called the 'prospect theory', a concept that showed how smart executives can make dumb decisions. Fear has been seen to distort perceived probability and undermined the rigour necessary for rational decision-making. Worse still, people did not necessarily understand what they were dealing with.

The worrying thing is that people don't keep track of their bad decisions. Gamblers do not try to learn from their mistakes; they're not about to spend time trying to figure out what they've done wrong. That's not an accident; they just don't want to know. How many of us have made a loss, chased it and chased it again and then it goes wrong again? No matter how bad it got for me I always thought it would get better – which is gambling at its worst extreme. I'd like to say that I've learned from my mistakes but I'm not so naive to believe that's true. I have to face the fact that I have a compulsive nature and I will always need to control it.

Pathological gambling is a hidden addiction. Unlike alcoholism there is no slurred speech or stumbling into work reeking of booze. Excessive gambling does not necessarily mean addiction as such but, as a general rule, healthy enthusiasms add to life whereas addictions take far too much from it. And, if it is taking anything from you that you can't afford, then it is unhealthy.

In a last-ditch, frenzied effort to repay their debts, gambling addicts often engage in criminal behaviour, such as forgery, embezzlement or fraud. When there are no further options left the person may suffer severe depression and have suicidal thoughts. At this stage they often reach rock bottom and it is only at this point that people tend to seek treatment. When I hit rock bottom, when there were no more roads to take, I went on the run and was eventually arrested at Frankfurt Airport about a week later. Unfortunately, hitting rock bottom can often be too late for certain parts of your lifestyle ay this stage – and is more often than not preceded by problems including divorce, absenteeism from work, family neglect and financial messes, including bankruptcy. There is also likely to be adverse health consequences including depression, insomnia, intestinal disorders, migraines and other stress-related illnesses. All of these affected me at one stage or another during my Barings period, culminating, I believe, in my diagnosis of colon cancer a few years later.

I never thought far enough ahead. I guess very few of us, especially men, really equate the risks that certain risk-based activities will put on our mental or physical well-being. We believe we are invincible – and that we will win out and succeed in the end. I learned the hard way, and I now know where to put controls and restrictions in place. I'm not sure that I can eradicate my compulsive and addictive personality but, as with a lot of things, improvement comes through awareness. And being aware of one's weaknesses is the key to finding solutions in many areas of one's life.

## IN CONVERSATION

### IVAN

When did you start to think you had a tendency towards addictive behaviour?

### NICK

I don't think it was too early in my life. My dad would watch the horses at the weekends which I thought was boring so I was put off that potential form of addiction at an early age. I'd want to watch something on a different channel but the horseracing would always take preference. I never ate chocolate until I was in prison and then only because it was all I could afford with the sixty pence I earned a week. My alcohol consumption would have been the first thing that showed a tendency to addictive behaviour – certainly in too much quantity from the age of sixteen, seventeen. It gave me food for thought as the ease with which I tended towards addictive behaviour with alcohol was a warning about trying anything else. I knew I had little control after I'd got so far into the behaviour – that scared me!

**IVAN**

What do you think is at the root of your addictive behaviour? For example, many people say they do what they do – binge drinking, gambling or whatever – to 'forget' themselves and thereby escape the burden of self-consciousness. Would that apply to you?

**NICK**

To a degree. If you asked me to describe myself in a couple of words, I'd suggest that I was shy and introverted. Aged sixteen, seventeen, going out and meeting people was always a bit easier after a couple of beers, which blunted the edges a little and generally made conversation a bit easier. While I would always have considered myself socially adept, that has mainly been with groups that are already formed and that I am comfortable with. A room full of strangers would have been very difficult for me to cope with years ago. After-dinner speaking has certainly taken me out of my shell in that respect. It's how I earn a living and there's an even greater need to be able to work the room.

**IVAN**

After-dinner speaking is a risk-taking activity and, once you get used to it, it is hugely good for self-confidence. But for the majority of people they would rather lose a limb than give a big speech. Public speaking is said to be one of the most stress-inducing and feared activities there is. The speaker knows he is putting himself on a pedestal and can be shot down, made to look an idiot, rejected. The feeling of risk in such circumstances comes about because of the need to be accepted by the wider community so as not to be made an outcast and thrown to the hyenas. But all risk taking is on a continuum and no one makes progress in the world without taking risks.

## NICK

Personally I believe that all behaviours exist on a continuum. Everyone takes risks but I took excessive risk. There was no happy medium with what I did at Barings. But my behaviour wasn't fundamentally different from someone taking a small risk.

## IVAN

Yes. Your career path put you in an environment where millions of pounds were at stake and the risks got bigger and bigger, each one a gamble.

## NICK

I don't think that I did what I did at Barings only because of my youth or lack of experience. I think there was an addictive element to it. When I was *making* money, I wanted to force it. When I was *losing* money and trading to try and get myself out of the mess, it was equally addictive so I would take on even more risk. Certainly around the periods where auditors and others were visiting and coming into the office, I forced those big trades and took on more and more financial risk. And that parallels the progression of any addictive behaviour. I think using credit cards, for example, is addictive.

## IVAN

That's an interesting thought, given the scale on which people rely on credit cards nowadays. Buying things certainly generates a short-term feeling of pleasure, something that our consumerist society depends on, and anything that gives pleasure can become addictive.

**NICK**

So spending credit will too! People are jumping from one credit card to another. I don't think it's widely acknowledged quite how addictive and damaging that can be. People have said I have an addictive personality. If I enjoy something, like playing poker, I can play it every night for a month. It would often see me up at first and then down and down and down. Eventually I'll stop playing and leave it alone. But I might go back to playing again a couple of months later. I see this addiction to risk and bluff as the same behaviour pattern I had at Barings, maybe because it *was* enjoyable. As you said, anything from which we gain enjoyment can be addictive. And that goes for drinking. I know people who religiously feel they have to go out every Friday and Saturday night with their mates and get drunk because it's the end of the week. They see this ritual as their reward.

Another way prison changed me is that I am now very comfortable with my own company. I no longer need to go out and be the centre of attention all the time.

**IVAN**

But you did when you were still trading. There is a type of person that has to turn the level of excitement and stimulus up in their brains just to feel awake and alive. Psychologists describe them as having 'low gain', a metaphor taken from sound systems. They are the sort who enjoy parties, love arguing and noise and excitement … and lots of sex. They would like adventure holidays and bunjee jumping! They think life is empty and boring without masses of stimulation. In contrast there are 'high-gain' people, whose inner 'noise' level is always turned up quite high and they get a lot of excitement out of thinking, reflecting and problem-solving. Reading a good book with a cup of tea in the evenings is enough to make them feel great. We all fit somewhere on this continuum and move up and down it a bit. Even people who like a lot of excitement will pull back sometimes and rest. And the outwardly calmest person will enjoy turning up the stimulation on occasion. My image of the world of trading floors, the Stock Exchange and money markets is it would attract low-gain people who like the buzz and excitement. It's a noisy, frenetic environment, isn't it?

**NICK**

Oh it is, yeah. And that's addictive, too! I'm not sure where I fit in on your high-gain/low-gain continuum though. I don't think either of the descriptions totally fits me. I'd suggest that I'm somewhere in the middle most of the time. I used to love going to work. I had a job I really enjoyed, that gave me a buzz I'm sure not everyone gets. And that was true throughout my time at Coutts and Morgan Stanley and then at Barings, which was for me the pinnacle of it because I was allowed on to the trading floor – the sharp end of what goes on within financial institutions. Trading was everything I aspired to because, before Barings, I'd been very much in the back office looking into the exciting trading floor world. I gave the traders high status in my own mind, maybe incorrectly, but it was the status that I to.

**IVAN**

You're still attracted to people of high status, aren't you? You like people that are at the top of their game.

**NICK**

Yes. Because achieving something is a quality I admire. Being successful is something I have always wanted to be. I'd love to have achieved more than I did in sport. I'd love to do something that I'd be remembered for, other than the collapse of the bank! Obviously that was the most negative and embarrassing thing that's happened in my life and unfortunately I will be remembered for it, but I'd love to achieve something that was positive.

**IVAN**

There is still time! You've not been idle. You did the psychology degree …

**NICK**

I did the psychology degree because I needed to put some structure back in my life after that first year back and being fairly hedonistic and having feelings that my life was empty. What I learned from prison was telling me that I was floundering without a structure to my days. I did have a very good job offer at the time but it meant moving to Holland, which didn't enthuse me greatly. I wanted to stay near family and friends.

**IVAN**

What sort of job offer?

**NICK**

Risk management, for an energy-trading company. When I decided not to take it I thought that doing a straight psychology degree would structure my life well enough while I sorted myself out long term.

**IVAN**

What did you like about the degree course?

**NICK**

It was a three-year course but the only things that really grabbed me while doing it were forensic psychology and health and occupational psychology. I could relate to those areas because of my own circumstances. Doing a degree also brought me a new group of friends and experiences. After the initial hard work of acclimatising to the life of a student, I enjoyed it. And again I was stretching myself. I enjoyed that challenge and I wanted to get a decent grade. I discovered I liked writing and I have some strong views on debt and how spending money is addictive and causes stress that I want to write about.

**IVAN**

Where did you actually live when you came back to England?

**NICK**

A friend and his wife offered me sanctuary. I lived a fairly hedonistic life for the first year when I got back: partying, meeting people, travelling around the country, having a good time. But my mood dropped every Monday. I hated Monday coming around.

**IVAN**

Why? Was it because people were going off to work and you weren't doing anything?

**NICK**

I don't think it was that. I think it was more personal. When I was in prison I never slept on a Sunday night. The lights would go off at nine o'clock and I'd toss and turn and just lie awake all night. The light would come on in the morning and I'd be tired all that day. I always put it down to the fact that for eight or nine years I'd been going to work on a Monday morning and I didn't have that routine any more. All my days were the same. Then, when I was released and had this very vibrant party life for a year, Monday tended to be quiet and it totally deflated me for a day. I would look back at the previous week and see myself slipping back into doing things that I did before the collapse of the bank: drinking a lot, blacking out, wasting money – three or four hundred pounds in a weekend. And I knew there were so many better uses for money than that. So after a while I regained control and stopped it. To be honest with you, that deflation on a Monday could have been me coming down from alcohol as well.

**IVAN**

I was thinking that.

**NICK**

That would certainly fit. If I were to drink on a Friday or Saturday night now, I'd still get that deflation on a Monday. It's quite difficult to shake it off. I know people who don't shake it off for two or three days after a binge. Sometimes alcohol is seen as a coping mechanism but it clearly isn't. It might deaden you for a while but it doesn't cure anything.

## IVAN

Fundamentally it's a depressant. It's just the first drink that still gives you a little bit of a lift by releasing inhibitions. The alcohol itself is poison that's quite hard for the brain to process.

## NICK

When I was at Barings, all the drinking I did each night just postponed the realisation of the losses I was making during the daytime. Postponing a depression! So it's not healthy and I do know people who have drink problems and some of them are close to me. It's an awful thing, and I'm not sure there is an adequate cure for it. You can't treat these people with kindness and it's very difficult to treat them with the harshness that might prompt them to change their behaviour themselves.

## IVAN

It amazes me how much effort is channelled into selling booze to people and legitimising alcoholism. A lot of British people today consider it normal behaviour for youngsters to go out and get absolutely plastered every Friday or Saturday night, causing long-term damage to their brains, livers and kidneys, which costs society a fortune.

**NICK**

But when you're eighteen or nineteen your powers of recovery are stronger ...

**IVAN**

They are. Up to a point. When we're young we feel immortal; that's part of the problem.

**NICK**

Speaking from experience, when somebody has a drink problem, they develop a spiral of repeating behaviours and it's exceptionally difficult to stop drinking. So you have to put the brake on early. You have to remain conscious. You have to be responsible. I studied alcoholism doing my psychology degree and it was one of the things that interested me from a health perspective. There were times when I would go out and binge drink and experience some of those lows symptomatic with drink dependency. I don't think that there is a preferred method of treating problem drinking that has a good success rate. To stop, one has to come to a kind of realisation about oneself. But how does one do that?

**IVAN**

There is a path that all addicts travel to free themselves from the addiction. It was discovered by studying how people on their own quit an addiction without the help of therapists. They went through stages very similar to the therapeutic process. The research showed that change is seldom a sudden event. Usually it follows predictable stages (*see* box). Most people mature out of addictions, even cocaine, once they start getting their needs met. But all addictions, if left untreated, will trigger depression eventually because the addictive behaviour fools people into believing they are getting their needs met in the real world, when actually the addictive behaviour is causing their lives to become more chaotic and dysfunctional. Both the addiction and the depression then need to be treated.

And addiction shortens lives.

## THE STAGES OF QUITTING AN ADDICTION

Psychologists James Prochaska and Carlo DiClemente conducted extensive research into addiction. Their 'Stages of Change' model, conceived in the late 1970s, has become a widely accepted formula for quitting all types of addiction:

- **Pre-contemplation:** people don't see themselves as having a problem, although other people may be well aware that they have a problem.

- **Contemplation:** the person begins to see cause for concern. They begin to have ambivalent feelings – wanting to change and not wanting to change.

- **Determination – a decision is made:** the turning point; the balance tips in favour of change. They may say something like, 'Something's got to change; I can't go on like this.' This stage is like a door or a window that opens up for a period of time. If the person goes through they can go to the next stage, otherwise they go back to an earlier stage.

- ▸ **Action:** the person chooses a strategy for change and pursues it. What is ordinarily thought of as treatment begins at this point.

- ▸ **Maintenance:** this is the effort required to maintain the change. It is not that hard to stop drinking, smoking or quit drugs, but maintaining that change is more difficult.

- ▸ **Relapse:** relapse is a common phenomenon; long-term follow-up shows that up to 90 per cent of clients treated for alcoholism will drink again at some time after treatment. A slip need not turn into a disastrous relapse. The challenge here is to recover from the slip or relapse as soon as possible by learning from each relapse what triggers it.

Many people may need to 'give up' more than once. The more these people go through the above cycle, the more they learn about the pattern and the more likely they are to succeed in the end in becoming addiction-free.

**NICK**

Definitely. I'm very conscious of that.

**IVAN**

I don't agree with you, however, that there are no preferred methods of treating problem drinking, or any other addictive behaviour for that matter. New discoveries about why *anyone* who doesn't get their emotional needs met is vulnerable to addiction, coupled with an understanding of what is happening in the brain to make one do things that are not in our long-term interests, are generating highly affective psychological treatments that help people. And research shows that some forms of therapy work much better than others, just as is the case in treating depression or post-traumatic stress disorder.

It's an odd thing, but there is little difference between the alcohol-drinking behaviour in research rats and our own. The standard drinking behaviour in reasonably contented laboratory rats is as follows: they often have an alcoholic drink before dinner; they also take a drink when it's freely available to them before they retire to bed at night and, every few weeks, they get together with their mates at the drinking fountain, and have a binge-drinking party. It turns out that the average drinker's behaviour is no different from a rodent's! Rats only become seriously addicted to alcohol when their innate needs ('rat givens') to roam, eat well, establish secure territory and mate is taken away from them. When the situation is reversed and they can get their needs met again, they revert to ordinary, relatively harmless, social drinking, just like humans. Even more remarkable is that, when these rats are given really large, natural ratlike territories to live in, where food is plentiful and there is no overcrowding stress, they hardly touch a drop.

**NICK**

So societies where we see a lot of addictive behaviour are ones that are preventing people getting innate needs met?

**IVAN**

Exactly. And people can become addicted to almost anything, not just the obvious things involving 'addictive substances', but almost any behaviour the imagination can dream up. This is because the human mind is able to create a much wider range of pleasurable expectations than a rat.

**NICK**

Food is another source of addictive behaviour. In terms of human lifespan the importance of diet cannot be understated.

**IVAN**

Eating less would help a lot of us Westerners live longer. We are eating too much.

**NICK**

I'm a bit overweight, although it might not be obvious. I could lose a fair amount of weight. When I went to Singapore I was 82 kilograms. I never used to do as much weight training as I do now but I was 82 kilograms, playing a lot of football, fairly fit, and could run any sort of distance. I'm 95 kilograms now. So I'm thirteen kilos heavier. That's two stone heavier than I was when I went to Singapore. But that's because there were steroid-type drugs in the chemotherapy, and I did bulk up a bit when I was in prison because of the physical strength exercises and running I did inside. I've run marathons since my release. My diet's never great. I like all the things that are bad for us! Fad diets aren't really for me.

**IVAN**

Anything that gives pleasure can become addictive behaviour if it is repeated compulsively to lift mood.

**NICK**

Some people have said I have an addictive personality.

**IVAN**

'Addictive personality' is just another term for 'greedy person'. We use jargon phrases like 'addictive personality' as a shield from blame because it makes it sound as if we cannot help ourselves. It makes it easier for us to excuse the fact that we are greedy. And ineffective psychiatrists and therapists like using it because it lets them off the hook for not being able to help someone. Some people are just greedier than others when satisfying their need for instant gratification and are too hedonistic to take responsibility for themselves. Addiction is greed without the brakes on.

THE GRIP OF ADDICTIVE BEHAVIOUR ▼

## HOW DO YOU KNOW IF YOU HAVE A SERIOUS PROBLEM?

If you answer 'yes' to all or nearly all of the following questions you have an addiction and may need help before it gets out of control:

- ▸ Do you spend a lot of time on your addictive activity – thinking about it as well as doing it?
- ▸ Do you overdo it, without realising or intending to?
- ▸ Do you need to engage in the activity more and more to get any satisfaction from it?
- ▸ Do you get withdrawal symptoms if you restrain yourself?
- ▸ Have you stopped your activity but substituted another addictive behaviour for it?
- ▸ Have you made at least a few attempts to quit?
- ▸ Has engaging in the activity badly affected other areas of your life?

# IVAN'S COMMENTARY

Around the world millions of people are caught up in self-destructive compulsive behaviours they wish they could stop. There are figures for the impact of some addictions such as the numbers who smoke, take hard drugs or drink to excess and the numbers who die from smoking, drug- and drink-related diseases each year. But for many we only have rough estimates: the numbers of people who work compulsively, eat compulsively, shop compulsively, have sex compulsively, self-harm compulsively, watch TV compulsively, have plastic surgery compulsively and a multitude of other activities. Many addictive behaviours are not obvious because they are socially accepted, such as addiction to having power and control over others.

In the UK, about a third of the adult – and a quarter of the teenaged – population smokes. At least six million men and three million women exceed the safe limits for alcohol. Half of British fifteen-year-olds drink alcohol regularly, consuming, on average, about ten units a week. Up to three per cent of the total UK population of fifteen to sixteen year olds use or have used heroin and up to four per cent of the same demographic use or have used crack or cocaine. One in seven people has tried cannabis, a drug that accounts for up to 80 per cent of illegal drug use. Around 13 million people have tried online poker, with £40m staked across at least 210 sites every day. Between one and two per cent of women in the UK are now estimated to suffer from sex addiction. A fifth of the population is dependent on caffeine. And so it could go on.

## THE COMMON CAUSE OF ALL ADDICTIONS

Any behaviour that intrinsically, or through conditioning, has the power to give us pleasure, can become addictive. We all have to eat, for example. And many people suffer from eating disorders. Psychotherapists approach this from a number of perspectives. These include seeing the disorder as an attempt by the sufferer to gain control of their life, or get attention, or to gain control of the family, or to avoid facing up to adult life or as a way of avoiding painful feelings from the past. No doubt there may be an element of truth in all these approaches. When you consider, however, that a person with an eating disorder is willing to risk their health, often their very life, in pursuit of this behaviour, it is that they are in the grip of a compulsive, addictive behaviour.

In one intriguing study anorexics were shown pictures of bodies of increasing thinness, reaching skeletal level, with their own head pasted over these bodies. They were all asked to choose the body shape they would consider thin enough. They all said that the bodies were all too fat. In other words it was the process of getting thinner that they were interested in, not any achievable goal.

The bulimic may wish to achieve the perfect body just as the addictive gambler wants to achieve economic freedom. What keeps them both addicted, however, is the excitement or change of mood associated with the 'acting out'. For the bulimic, the thinking about bingeing, the planning of the binge, the buying of the food, the eating of the food, and then throwing it up, all produce an increasing intensification of emotional experience.

The same is true for the shopaholic, the sexaholic and the workaholic. It is the emotional intensity – 'the high' – that all addicts are chasing. Bulimics may say they don't even taste most of the food they binge on. This may well be true, but there is an emotionally intense state associated with eating that the addictive part of the personality is chasing. It is well known that starvation can also create intense feelings of satisfaction. These may be derived from a feeling of power and control over oneself or others, and feelings of purity and goodness. Starvation may also stimulate the production of endorphins, feel-good chemicals released by the body in response to pain. Endorphins are natural opiates and seem to reinforce addictive behaviours.

In the early stages of addictive behaviour, a person is trying to increase feelings of pleasure by manipulating their feelings through carrying out certain behaviours. These behaviours may become progressively more a part of their life. The 'high' they cause may begin to dominate their psychology. Even when the person is not indulging in the behaviour, a lot of their time may be taken up with thinking about doing it, or resisting doing it. The person begins to develop the disastrous and erroneous belief that the real satisfaction and meaning of life lies in their 'highs' caused by 'acting out' the addictive behaviour.

This is the stage when the desire for the emotional intensity caused by the addictive process dwarfs the addict's need for intimacy and closeness with others. The addict is now using people and his main 'relationship' in life has become with the addictive behaviour. In the final stages of addiction, the behaviour becomes a compulsive ritual indulged in to avoid withdrawal symptoms and the addict's relationship with those closest to him is in trouble. His family and friends sense their loss of contact with the real person. They also sense that they are being used. All kinds of denial, lying and cover-ups then become an entrenched part of the addict's lifestyle. The noose of addiction progressively chokes off access to the healthy part of the addict's personality and physical and mental health problems arise making the addict's denial of his self-destructive lifestyle harder to sustain.

> The addict has now programmed himself to believe that: intimacy = intensity of emotional response

True intimacy, of course, springs from feelings of being understood and accepted and sharing experiences with another human being. It ranges in expression from moments of intensity to moments of silent togetherness. A composer doesn't limit himself only to high notes when he creates a beautiful composition. If we allow ourselves to become addicted to emotional intensity, we distort the functioning of the mind/body. Indeed, it has been attested throughout the ages by people of wisdom that the most meaningful states of consciousness and well-being are more likely to be experienced by people who lead non-addictive, non-self-centred, emotionally balanced lives.

Addictions are not diseases with neat physical causes, despite the finding of genetic elements to conditions such as alcoholism. Any successful ex-smoker, for instance, will know that the most uncomfortable aspect of giving up smoking is psychological, not physical. This is so, even with such drugs as heroin.

We all know people who drink or take drugs too much during a bad phase in their lives, we may even have done so ourselves – after a divorce, a redundancy or other major upset. We are most vulnerable at those times when we lose our moorings. The phase in life where this happens and people drift and feel rudderless – and are willing to try anything – is when we are young. For some groups of adolescents and young adults, drug or alcohol abuse is almost an obligatory rite of passage. But in most cases, no matter how bad the addiction seems at the time, people recover from such a phase without too much difficulty when they move on to the next stage in their lives and get their needs met in more natural ways. They mature out of it.

## THE GREAT ADDICTION MYSTERY

The puzzling question is, why does nature, which used so much intelligence in evolving human beings to be the most creative and adaptive creature on this planet, make us so vulnerable to addiction? Why do so many of us wilfully indulge in self-destructive behaviour at the risk of damaging relationships, our children and our work prospects? Why do we let addictions make us behave immorally, against all the principles held prior to the addiction – stealing, criminal activity etc? At first sight it seems incredible that nature could have allowed this apparent design flaw to exist.

The solution has been found by looking closely at the mechanism in the brain that gets 'perverted' by addictive behaviour. This mechanism, built into all life forms, is highly adaptive, but it's led awry in addiction. The mechanism is this: for any experience or activity that the brain approves of, it gives you a feeling of pleasure when you carry it out. It does this because, as far as the brain is concerned, the activity is helping you get one of your fundamental needs met. However, the brain doesn't continue to give you the same amount of pleasure every time you repeat that experience; otherwise, you would not move on. You would not progress; you wouldn't go out and seek other experiences and learn new knowledge that might stand you in good stead if suddenly the environment changed and your usual sources of nourishment were withdrawn. Brains have to have a way of encouraging creatures to stretch themselves – to explore, experience differences, learn, develop new skills – so they can adapt to environmental changes. So, once we have mastered some new experience, the brain withdraws the high degree of pleasure from the process. But the brain still wants to maintain that knowledge, experience or skill, so what it does is give you pain if you stop doing it. If you decide to start taking exercise on a regular basis, for example, and you walk three miles each evening; the first few times you feel better for it. You are getting fit and it is very pleasurable. After a while, though, it starts to become a routine experience – you don't get quite the same pleasure out of doing it. Yet, if you stop doing it, you feel something is missing, something is not quite right. You feel bad about slobbing around in the evening instead of walking.

So that is the 'stick' the brain uses to goad you into maintaining the behaviour it approves of. Once it withdraws the pleasure aspect it can now use pleasure for a new behaviour or challenge that you need to reach for. By judicious use of the 'carrot and the stick', it helps you to maintain what you have achieved (with the stick of painful withdrawal symptoms), and continues rewarding you (with the carrot of pleasure) when you stretch yourself in new ways that will further your development. It is a wonderful mechanism that evolved to enable life, from single-celled organisms onwards, to progress. However, in chemical addiction, this process (which is generally so highly adaptive) goes disastrously wrong. The reason is that, when we ingest an addictive chemical, it hijacks the very same chemicals the brain uses for rewarding us, that make us feel good. When we pump them in from outside, pleasurable feelings are released in the brain and, as that experience is repeated, the mechanism that we have just described, cancels out that pleasure.

Then, if we want to get more pleasure, we have to increase the dosage of the drug. But, if we stop taking the drug at any point, the 'stick' comes in – we get withdrawal symptoms. So that is the 'carrot and the stick' – we keep taking more of the drug to get the carrot and, if we stop taking it, we get the stick. Hence, developing addicts find that they have to take more and more of the drug to get any pleasure, and find it harder to stop because of the pain of withdrawal; thus, they have to commit increasingly to the drug-dependent lifestyle.

For most people who start to overindulge in some pleasurable activity – say taking in substances like alcohol – as they mature and learn how to get their emotional needs met more effectively through relationships, taking on responsibilities, work, building a family etc. they realise that the pleasures that arise from getting these essential needs met naturally are being interfered with, blunted, by too much drinking. They realise there is a conflict and so they cut back on the alcohol in order to maintain pleasure elsewhere in their lives. In other words there is a natural counterweight to overindulgence in any appetite built in to us. If we overindulge in one pleasure we interfere with others, and that provides the motivation to keep any single pleasure from getting out of hand and dominating our lives.

So nature has built this lovely balance into us. But there is another complication: not everybody is equally vulnerable to developing an addiction. The vulnerable are those who do not have their counterweight to addiction in place: having their essential life needs (the human givens) met. They tend to be lonely, isolated or are the suddenly bereaved who have lost a life partner or who are young with no responsibilities and therefore no way to generate the self-esteem that comes from being involved in work, building a family and being involved in meaningful community activities. Many of them lack relationship skills or don't know how to manage their anxiety and stress other than through taking drugs or drink. Some have been traumatised in war or been subject to violent attacks or sexual abuse. Any such cause can damage human beings and make them vulnerable to addiction.

It might seem that this doesn't always apply. What about high achievers who reach a stage in life where they have great wealth, a family and, to all intents and purposes, seem successful, but then become addicts. They are not 'down and outs' or social failures. But the carrot and stick principle still applies. If they no longer get pleasure, a healthy, natural reward, from having to stretch themselves to build their career, for example, they start to try and put pleasure back by drinking too much or indulging in other pleasures excessively, with all the consequent damage.

Whatever the cause, the first step in combating an addiction is to help the person to recognise that they have one. They must come to recognise that this behaviour, in the overall economy of their life, is causing them more pain than pleasure. This is done by calming them down and not being too critical. (If you criticise or argue with an addict, all you succeed in doing is driving them back into their 'emotional brain' and black and white thinking.) In a sympathetic, supportive way you help them to look at how destructive the addiction is in their life, how it's creating an emotional wasteland leading to nowhere except an early grave.

With the right kind of therapy most addicts can be fairly quickly rescued from their predicament.

# chapter 9
# FREEDOM AND A NEW
# LIFE – a positive start

## NICK'S STORY

The third of July 1999 had been firmly fixed in my mind for the last three and a half years of my sentence. As soon as the judge had handed down my term I had known exactly when I was going to be released. I think they'd even mentioned it to me when I was passing through the administrative part of the prison, transiting from remand to the fully incarcerated part of the jail. As I was starting my sentence, the only other English prisoner in Tanah Merah was making his way to the gallows. My cell had been his while he was on remand but thankfully our sentences had set us on very different paths. My spell in the punishment cells would normally have prolonged my stay by a number of days, but I don't think anyone wanted to disappoint the waiting media horde. The initial euphoria of finally having a date to aim for had been offset by the stark reality of the conditions I was going to have to endure. My first day in the main part of the prison was in the 'gangster' hall, the wing inhabited by the criminal law detainees.

They were a scary bunch. Just as in a game of monopoly they had gone to jail without passing go or, in this case, court. They were placed in jail on suspicion of serious crimes and, although they'd never been tried and convicted, their cases were reviewed yearly. Many were held there on suspicion of murder; none of them had a date for release. The majority of these guys had already been in prison for close to fifteen years; these were the desperados of Tanah Merah. And then there was me – a white-collar criminal mixed up with the so-called cream of the Singaporean underworld. It was important to hold my own and that's what I did – tenuously at times, but somehow I managed to get through it.

My last day was a form of a torture in itself. Usually one leaves the prison gates behind you first thing in the morning but nothing was straightforward with my case. At the twelfth hour they informed me I'd be staying till closer to midnight and that I'd have to destroy all the diaries that had kept me company over the last three and a half years. The day dragged on like no other. At five o'clock I was locked back up in my cell, with a dog-eared football magazine for amusement. At ten o'clock I was taken to the administration area, informed that I was banned from Singapore for life and handed a small box that held all my possessions. This was all that was left of what I owned in the world. Everything I had owned in Singapore was either still held there by the liquidators or had been given back to Lisa. Everything I had owned in England had either been sold or had gone to Lisa. What lay in front of me represented my worldly possessions: a few letters, magazines I hadn't been allowed to read and some clothes. These now had to be compressed into a small holdall that weighed no more than seven kilos, so that I could gain easy access to the plane.

Heathrow didn't look any different when I got back to the UK – not that I had much time to take it in. From the moment I left the plane until I was spirited away, my speedy departure masterminded by a lovely driver named Roger, I was surrounded by photographers trying to snatch a shot and journalists eager for a quote. They'd be squatting down in front of me, leaning out of corridors and, more often than not, I'd walk straight into them. This was my first real brush with the British media. I'd seen my name in print, seen some of the pictures but never really been at the sharp end of where it all happened. I'd left Britain an unknown employee, and didn't have a clue as to the kind of attention anyone famous or infamous is subjected to. Stephen, my lawyer, was there as always, far more respectful than me as I bulldozed my way towards the hotel room that offered me temporary sanctuary. I felt a mixture of elation and fear, seesawing between the two, as I really had no idea what the next minute held, let alone the next hour or day. It was all thoroughly planned out: Stephen had been busy making sure that my return passed with almost military precision. As always, my protection was his priority.

My driver looked goggle-eyed at my baggage as he smuggled me into his car and joked about waiting for the additional bags to be delivered – he was convinced I had some money stashed somewhere.

I arrived back in the early hours of Sunday morning to pick up the first English newspaper I had seen in years. I was struck by how relatively devoid of news it was. I was probably the only person in England who didn't know who Jordan was, and was certainly the least interested in what she was doing and what she was or wasn't wearing. Celebrity was bigger than the news itself! Perhaps that explained the interest that surrounded my return from Singapore and why there were so many people trying to throw money at me. A deal was done with the *Daily Mail* for an exclusive series of interviews and pictures. Naturally they were worried about stories being leaked to other newspapers and somebody sneaking a picture so, rather bizarrely, family and friends would have to meet Roger at a service station ten miles away and then follow him back to the house we were staying at. This characterised my first week of freedom. That and takeaway meals and an endless supply of champagne and beer.

Freed from the shackles of Singapore, it was very easy to revert to type. My taste buds were reignited and I wanted to consume everything I could as soon as I could. I had an appetite that was difficult to satiate. Roger would disappear into the nearest town and return with an assortment of takeaway food. On one occasion he went missing for hours; it transpired that the Indian restaurant we'd ordered food from was so astounded by a takeaway order of over £200 that they were plying Roger with free beers. We eventually got the food but Roger could barely walk.

At the time I hated that first week. I was free in name only and didn't really have my freedom until the week after. I'd had four and a half years of being told what to do and I resented the constraints that were being placed upon me now. My immediate reaction was to rebel, argue as much as I could but, much the same as happened in prison, it got me nowhere. The liquidators basically owned a part of me and everything had to be vetted by them. They were now my warders.

Broken English had plagued me for the last three and a half years, so much that I think I became difficult to understand back in the country of my birth. I'd had to adapt. I could now swear fluently in Chinese, Malay and Indian. I didn't use it often but it was important to know when it was being aimed in my direction. Fresh home from Singapore I found myself talking slowly and really trying to stress the important parts of the sentence; a throwback to trying to converse with the other prison inmates. Most of the cellmates I was made to share with had rudimentary English at best. Initially it caused a few strange looks but it wasn't long until I was back in the swing of things and my normal estuary English was slipping off my tongue. Nothing pleased me more than, on my first visit to London, stepping into a cab and hearing, 'Where to, Guv?' I silently thought, anywhere will do, mate, as long as it's not prison. I was home and very, very glad to be there.

Obviously there was a sexual need that hadn't been met for the last four years. That was high on the agenda of things to do quickly after my release from Singapore! Initially, instant and easy satisfaction was the order of the day for me, rather than anything lasting or meaningful. I was quite cynical about what my new found notoriety might mean to people and was very wary of getting hurt, so I remained aloof about everything. That need met, I then had to apply my mind to sifting through the many offers I had for my services. I had to find something that wasn't going to upset the liquidators or creditors too much and wasn't asking me to do anything too stupid. A position in a bank may have given the liquidators a job for life but I wasn't going near any of them. A bizarre array of offers came my way, including ad work –

for instance, for board games. The most obvious avenue for earning a living was after-dinner speaking, although this had the potential to be an 'out of the frying pan and into the fire' situation. After removing all that stress from my life, the only real income avenue left open to me carried a lot of fear with it. I would probably be described as an accomplished speaker now but that wasn't always the case. I was shot with nerves for my first engagement and still feel a little like that before each event. It's important to get a laugh early on in the speech; that is usually quite easily done recalling an introduction by a very dear friend of mine, Russ Kane, who once introduced me as the only person to write a cheque and the bank bounces.

## IN CONVERSATION

### IVAN

So, you survived and you were out. How did that feel?

### NICK

Every day for four and a half years I'd looked forward to getting out. In a way, that whole period, from the first day I arrived in Singapore, was coming to an end – seven and a half years. Release meant I could put the whole sorry mess behind me. Strangely I had a taste of how release felt when I was first arrested.

### IVAN

Was that because you no longer had to hold the fiction together?

**NICK**

Yes. The three years of lying and rogue trading, the pretending to everybody, the role-playing, were over. The end was in sight at last, even though I knew I would have a prison sentence to get through. It wasn't such a bad thing when the plane landed at Frankfurt Airport and the German border police made the special journey out to the steps of the plane to arrest me. Potentially the most difficult part lay ahead but the amount of time I was going to have to stay in jail had limits. The important thing was to set about defining those limits.

**IVAN**

I bet that was a huge weight off your mind!

**NICK**

It was, and when I was finally freed the whole terrible seven-and-a-half-year period was done with. That doesn't necessarily please everybody. I'm sure there are people who would love me to be saying sorry for the rest of my life. I'm not going to do that. I've been truly remorseful for what happened. I've paid some pretty heavy penalties and have to grasp the second chance I have been given. As soon as I could quantify how long my sentence was going to be, I had a target. I think definite targets are important. I could chisel away at the time that I had to serve and hopefully be left with something to look forward to after my release. It was hard work – a six-and-a-half-year sentence is an immeasurably long period of time when you are locked up 23 hours a day but you can get through it if you set your mind to it. I'd start thinking in terms of the number of months that I had to pass and then as things got more manageable would pass this into weeks and then days. With a date you have something to aim for, something to achieve. I looked forward to being released from the first day that I was in prison. Again, going back to the human givens, it is about stretching yourself to reach that target.

## IVAN

We all need clear goals.

## NICK

I counted down to my release date as soon as I got it. I never knew what was waiting for me when I came out but I was very close to my lawyer, who became a very great friend. He was exceptionally good to me throughout the prison sentence. He was always honest about what was ahead of me and what I could expect and that kept me in the right frame of mind. He grounded me in realism, never promised me things he couldn't deliver and that really helped me along. I look for that myself in people whenever I have any sort of professional transaction to complete. When I was released it was difficult to make decisions at first, difficult to equate all the side-effects of a particular decision so, more often than not, I'd be on the phone to Stephen looking for advice. Most people I find – lawyers, salesman, builders, even doctors – tell you what they think you want to hear. That's no use to anyone; telling the truth may lose you the transaction but will earn you more respect in the long run.

**IVAN**

Was there a moment in prison when you decided to try and live your life more honestly from then on?

**NICK**

I thought about it a lot. I think that what happened with me and Barings could have sucked many ordinary averagely honest people in. My honesty and integrity were severely tested early on and I failed those tests. I hid the losses and ultimately cheated the bank out of millions of pounds. I betrayed the trust of everyone at the bank but I was in a situation that with hindsight I know I wasn't ready for. I didn't have the necessary management skills or the expertise to deal with the situation at hand. I'm told that many people in the city can imagine themselves doing what I did. Some friends of mine are convinced that if it was them in a similar situation they would have ended Barings in far more spectacular style and in much less time!

**IVAN**

Had you done anything dishonest before?

**NICK**

I'd fiddled my expenses, but I think that's something many people do. There were times when I'd go out to dinner in Indonesia with friends and the bill would find its way on to my expense sheet when it shouldn't have. But Barings were grateful for the work that we were doing out there at the time, so they were more than willing to pay it. But now I find it horrible to be on record as a dishonest person. Wanting to live my life more honestly pretty much colours everything I do now, with my wife, my family and with my friends and colleagues. The whole tissue of lies I built up over the three years before the collapse of the bank was the most damaging thing I've ever done to myself in and I don't want to do that again. As I was writing about my experiences in prison, things I had done were coming back to me, I confronted them on paper. An underlying theme became working out ways I could improve myself as a person, become better and treat people in a nicer way. Gradually my outlook on life changed, for the better I'd like to think, but sometimes too much honesty can scare people as well. My attitude to money changed, it had to. But even in the first year of my release I wasn't putting into practice the things that I wanted to do. It was a pretty hedonistic first year – lots of travel, partying and drinking. But every Monday I'd wake with a real empty feeling, rueing all of the money I'd spent at the weekend and thinking I could have done so much more with it. That had to change.

One of my sisters is a single mother struggling with three children. When I looked back on things I had done in Singapore I was ashamed. For example, there was an awards dinner with an important customer over from America attending. I ended up buying 24 bottles of Krug champagne in a nightclub. It cost me $11,000! I just had no sense of the value of money at that time. None at all! I remembered that and felt disgusted with myself because it was just a complete waste. There are so many better ways that I could have used that money. I didn't get any enjoyment out of it. I probably woke up with another blackout hangover.

Remembering such events brought home the value of money to me. When I came back from Singapore, I got far more enjoyment out of my nephew than an expensive bottle of champagne. My nephew kick-boxes for England and he's very successful. He started when he was eight and when I came back to England I took him along to training and competitions. I paid a fairly small amount of money for him to go every month and that has far greater value for me now. I'd rather do that than go out and spend money on myself. That's still very true now with Mackensey and my stepchildren, Kersty and Alex. I have no problem going without so that they can have something they need. So that's an example of something that I wanted to change. I found myself wanting to do things for other people.

**IVAN**

No one progresses as a human being unless they serve others without getting secondary gains for themselves in doing so.

**NICK**

What sort of secondary gains?

**IVAN**

Well, some people do good deeds because it makes them feel good, or feel morally superior or to get attention. It gives them an emotional, pious high. It seems to me that strong emotions are the bane of humankind. We need them but they can so easily harm us.

**NICK**

Yes, it was interesting what you said earlier about men not trusting their emotions. I'm not highly emotional; I'm on an even keel most of the time, but there are things I feel strongly about. Leona's and my family is exceptionally important to me. I see films on TV where somebody is suffering from an illness, or from some kind of loss, and relate to them because of my own suffering. It will bring a tear to my eye. Those are the occasions when I think about dying. I had a life-threatening illness and I never consider myself as recovered. I'm not *struggling* with cancer: I'm *living* with it. That's the way that I like to phrase it. When I was reading for my degree I found out that most people who get cancer can often pre date the start of their illness by a couple of years. It usually coincides with a highly stressful period in their lives.

**IVAN**

Stressful life events concerning loss are linked to cancer. In your case you lost your wife *and* your freedom.

**NICK**

*And* my status.

**IVAN**

And status. You had so many losses, one after the other, and that is exactly what researchers find in a higher proportion of people with cancer than in healthy people.

**NICK**

The *Financial Times* described me as a robot because of the matter-of-fact way I talk about the collapse of the bank and prison life. But they are things I've dealt with.

Dying, by contrast, isn't. It frightens me. I'm not conventionally religious, though I do believe there is some higher purpose to our lives. But I don't accept things blindly. I need to experience things, see something tangible and be able to gain knowledge and information from something direct, and then make my own decisions. So 'God' and an afterlife, for me are a leap of faith too far. The Bible is full of good stories, but that could be all there is in it as far as I'm concerned. But my fear of dying is strong and one of the stressors I still have. One reads and hears about people becoming more comfortable or at peace with the fact of their inevitable death as they get older, but I can't ever imagine myself feeling like that. I really can't, although I know we're all getting older day by day. I just want to experience so much, especially with the new baby. So I'm not unemotional.

### IVAN

It's a wise person who keeps in mind that each hour could be his last. We are more alive when we remember that life can be taken away from us at any moment. But *fear* of dying is just like worrying and depression: an unnecessary extra problem on top of everything else. If you get depressed because you've been made redundant, for example, you've not only got the problem of what you're going to do for money, you've also got the depression, an extra layer of suffering that doesn't help you get another income. We're all going to die but adding an extra emotional layer – fear – on top of that inevitability is just as absurd as adding depression to a problem, because we're going to have to face death anyway. The real issue is how we prepare ourselves for it.

**NICK**

When I was first diagnosed with cancer, that word for me was heavily associated with death. That's not true any more. But I did think about dying a lot and it was one of the things I couldn't deal with at the time. Today though, every so often, something triggers those thoughts again, usually when I'm watching something a little bit moving on the telly about somebody who's died of or is suffering with cancer. I love happy endings, but *true-life* happy endings. A happy ending in a movie doesn't really do much for me, but real people who have overcome adversity – illness, poverty, rejection – to succeed in what they're doing, in sport or business or whatever, does. I'm not quite the emotionally dead character that some of the newspapers have portrayed me as.

**IVAN**

If you *were* emotionally dead you wouldn't have suffered from stress: stress is about strong emotions. The desire to succeed, which you still have, is also a strong emotion. As is to love your family.

**NICK**

I still have all of those desires. It's just that they're not what I talk about.

**IVAN**

How did you adapt to freedom again?

**NICK**

Stephen helped me a lot. He was there to deal with the liquidators. He was there for the trial. He became a close friend and, if my sisters or the family needed money or

anything, he was the point of contact. In many ways he
metaphorically took my role within the family as the oldest child. So he was my rock I relied on in prison. When I
was diagnosed with cancer he was my conduit for the
Embassy, for any member of my family, for my friends;
he'd bring messages. It was he who came back with me on
the plane when I was released and didn't know what the
future held, or even the next few hours. All I knew was
that it was going to be better than the last four and a half
years. Although my future was unclear, I felt positive
about it. I didn't have a sense of desperation in not knowing what might happen. Before, when there were plenty
of negatives around, I was always looking for that
'definite'. Having my freedom back was so positive I felt I
could cope with anything. I just went with the flow. When
I got back, however, I was given an injunction for £100
million as soon as I stepped off the plane, which kind of
put a bit of dampener a on it. But it didn't really bother
me because I didn't have any money. When you've got
nothing, you've got nothing to lose.

**IVAN**

Why did you get an injunction?

**NICK**

There had been stories in the newspapers – again, completely false – about me having millions stashed away in a
secret bank account. I was supposed to have shared these
deepest secrets with one of my inmates in prison. Now,
considering that I didn't tell a soul about my trading at
Barings over a period of three years, the chances of me
blabbing something to a relative stranger seems a bit

absurd. A couple of English newspapers had advertised in the *Straits Times* for stories about me; they were paying money and got what they wanted – a story. The gutter press at its finest.

**IVAN**

So what assets did you actually have?

**NICK**

When I came back?

**IVAN**

Yes. In round figures. A lot of people will ask, 'Well, what's he actually talking about?' What about savings or investments?

**NICK**

My wife had disposed of two houses we owned in the UK, so I had a little money in bank accounts that I knew I was to be allowed to access on a drip-down basis to live on.

**IVAN**

What about the remains of bonuses paid by Barings?

**NICK**

There was some money. The *Daily Mail* paid me a six-figure sum for an article when I got back. It was used partly to pay legal fees and partly to pay the liquidators. But I would have said that the entirety of what I was worth was eighty or ninety thousand pounds.

**IVAN**

So you weren't rich?

## NICK

Not at all. The money I earned with the *Daily Mail* article all went. I never saw any of it. The movie never earned me a penny. The total revenue from the book approached a million pounds in advances. The English advance was substantial and foreign nights were sold to Germany, to Japan, to pretty much every country in the world. But that just paid legal fees. I had a German lawyer and English and Singaporean lawyers who weren't cheap. None of that remains. The plane coming back to London was full of media people trying to get 'Nick Leeson' stories. Two of these people had written the first article about me having five million stashed away and it was that that caused the injunction to be taken out. One of them cheekily asked me for my autograph in a book. Stephen whispered to me, 'That's the guy who wrote the piece that's causing all the trouble.' So I said, 'Tell him to stick the book up his arse then. I'm not signing it!' The injunction wasn't a joke, but defining the value on it was, because I didn't have any money. When Stephen said, 'Well, what figure do we put on it?' I said, 'I don't care. You can put a billion on it. Ten billion. A trillion. It doesn't really matter because I haven't got it.' Nobody's going to find an account with serious money deposited in it because it just doesn't exist. It was ludicrous. So it was fixed at £100 million and I had to agree to put a certain amount of monthly earnings against it.

Throughout the whole process, the journey back, everything, Stephen was always there. To have someone I could rely on and talk to and get advice from was invaluable because after four and a half years in prison I found it hard to make decisions. He was my decision-maker. I'd phone him up and say, I've got this or that opportunity, and he'd think about it, and whether it could be misinterpreted, and help me decide. In prison there are not many opportunities to think in that way. They do your thinking for you. The guards turn the lights on at six in the morning. You have a shower at seven because the water's turned off at eight. They give you a piece of bread at half-past eight. You get out for an hour and you run round the yard. You come back. You exercise. And, if you get the opportunity, you bathe again, you then do a mixture of sleeping and reading before the lights are turned off, and it starts all over again the next day. I lived that monotonous life for four years and four months.

**IVAN**

So he was a sort of coach to help you get back in the swing of life?

**NICK**

That's what he was for the first six to eight weeks – a life coach, if you like. Whatever happened in my life he was my point of referral. The first week I was with the *Daily Mail,* that was surreal. I had two reporters with me all the time asking questions and having conversations. They were writing the stories they wanted to write in the paper and we had people transcribing what we were talking about. It was a strange existence. Family and friends came to see me, and some of them stayed overnight. After a week I relocated back to Watford, a place that has always been good to me. The journalists joked that it was always difficult to get a story out of anybody from Watford. People didn't easily give stories or photos to the media about me. There was mutual respect between myself and everybody I knew there. They're all still friends to this day and we often see each other. So moving back to Watford was moving back home, although there was some stress involved because journalists kept following me around. I went out to a nightclub one evening with some friends soon after I was back and we were having a few drinks. I was wearing a new pair of shoes. I hadn't worn shoes for four and a half years in prison so my feet were in agony and I had to take them off in the nightclub and walk around in my socks. This was reported in the *Daily Telegraph* like major news. I was described dancing barefoot in the nightclub. Everyone who knew me could tell it wasn't an accurate story because I don't dance. Perhaps the fact that I was dancing was the real headliner! So there were some stresses in relocating. But it was a great homecoming from people, many of whom had been writing to me in prison.

**IVAN**

That must have helped you survive, knowing you had friends.

**NICK**

To a degree my emotional needs were being met even while I was in prison. I can see that now. Having friends was the key. There is a cliché about people leaving prison getting depressed when they re-enter society as they try to come to terms with all the changes and find it difficult. I never experienced that, and I think those letters were what helped me to bridge the gap. There were technological advances I noticed when I got out, even after four and a half years. Email and the use of the Internet and mobile phones had come on massively and I had to get up to date with all that. But I didn't have a problem getting on a bus or train. And I never felt I was shunned by society, because I wasn't. Everyone important to me – friends and the family – had kept in constant touch throughout my imprisonment. So I had no fear. I hit the ground running and have got on with my life.

**IVAN**

You haven't just got into the swing of things after coming out of prison; you've got yourself into a new marriage and had your first baby and become a stepdad for your wife's two fabulous children.

**NICK**

My life has done a massive about-turn since I left prison. It is very positive now and I take a great deal of comfort from that. I no longer do things to excess. I don't waste money like I once did. Memories of my profligacy often come back, especially when I go back to Asia. Two years ago in the summer I sat on a beach in Hua Hin, which is between Saigon and Hanoi in Vietnam. Little kids were working so hard selling stuff on the beach just to get an education. They really beavered away to get the money they needed: £15 for a six-month period in school. They're lovely kids with such a sunny disposition. And then, in Cambodia, I saw kids living out of dustbins, leading lives of abject squalor. It really did force the message home. One can't help everybody, again my realism kicks in, but I wasted so much money, and part of my life as well, to a degree.

**IVAN**

When did you meet Leona?

**NICK**

While doing the degree. I was probably more taken with her than she was with me and it was me that did most of the chasing. I proposed to Leona after a fairly short period and for the first six months it was a case of getting to know her children. She has two: Alex is five now and Kersty is ten. Leona will tell you how important it was for her that I could fit and be accepted into Kersty and Alex's lives. It was a new and challenging time for me. And stressful because I'm always worrying about how they're reacting to me. The age difference between them means their reactions to me are different. And I want to do everything right by them.

**IVAN**

How does Leona think you're shaping up as a dad?

**NICK**

You'd have to ask her. But I think I do OK. I'm a little bit harder on the children about getting their school studies moving along than Leona is, probably because of the values my mother instilled in me when I was young. But I don't go to the extremes that my mother did, though I do think it's necessary that children receive a good education.

There is one thing that does worry me about becoming a stepfather: my name does bring with it a lot of baggage. If you look in most modern economics, business or law books, the Barings case features in all of them. The Barings collapse is studied right up to postgraduate level.

So, throughout their educational career, my children are probably going to see my name, their surname, in the context of me being 'a disgraced banker' or 'rogue trader'. A close friend, who I was at university with, has two teenage children. They live in Sheffield. His fourteen-year-old son was having an economics class at school one day and the teacher was detailing the collapse of Barings and passed a remark about my role in the collapse of the bank and characterised me as this less-than-nice person. And he stood up in the class and said, 'That's not entirely true. I know him and he is a nice person.' And I can see that kind of incident happening in the future with my own children involved and it's a constant worry. Mackensey, who is four days old as we speak, is totally oblivious to his daddy now, but he will learn. His experiences of me initially will be as his dad, but later he's going to come across some nasty stuff that other kids will also find out about, and we all know how kids at school can be a bit hurtful.

**IVAN**

Not necessarily. Perhaps in another ten years the Barings collapse will become an historical event as opposed to a terrible scandal.

**NICK**

I don't think so. I deal with everything with total realism. To the day I die, unless I reinvent myself somehow or achieve something else which deflects some of that attention, I will be known as 'the rogue trader' and 'disgraced banker'. I am very conscious of that and I still flinch at the mention of my name and some of the descriptions that precede and follow it and I worry about how that will impact on people who are close to me. For four and a half years in the Singapore prison I was fortunate, although I didn't realise it at the time, that I was completely kept away from the media's attention. My family and friends had to cope with that and it must have been extremely difficult and painful to read some of the things that were said about me. They had to deal with it without being able to liaise with me and hear my side of the story. My father had journalists and TV cameras arriving on his doorstep and sticking cameras in his face and he'd never experienced anything like that in his life before. None of us had. So he was thrust into the limelight of this ever-developing story that they had no real knowledge about. And it must have been very difficult for him and my family and friends to cope with. And I am very grateful to them for it.

**IVAN**

What was your dad's attitude to all this?

**NICK**

It's summed up by the fact that he punched one of the *Mirror* journalists on his doorstep. Not a bad thing to do really, under the circumstances! But I think it was beyond his comprehension, to be honest with you.

**IVAN**

Do you talk about what happened when you're with your family?

## NICK

I don't think we've spoken about it at all. But then I don't
speak to a great number of people about it. I probably
speak more freely to people that I don't know than people
that I do know. It's one of those strange, quirky things of
human nature. It's easier to talk to strangers sometimes
than the people that are closest to you, especially if they're
hurting a bit too. The same thing happens with anybody
who suddenly suffers from a life-threatening illness or
other life-changing event. Rather than talking, it can
sometimes be better to write down your needs on a piece
of paper and ask them to help you without having an
emotional conversation about it. Could you do this for
me, could you do that for me, could you ask such and
such to do that for me? They love to help you but sometimes just asking for what you want them to do is
difficult. That's my experience of it.

## IVAN

I think that is good way for most men to handle it,
definitely. Writing it down is a good idea. It may not work
so well for women though, because they have a bigger
need to talk and express their emotions.

## NICK

So, in terms of relationships, we don't talk seriously about
Barings, prison and the cancer. We do joke about it,
though. Whenever I'm out and we're talking about
money, perhaps in a restaurant, I always say that Leona
looks after the bank account! But it's all tongue in cheek.
And I like having a laugh. Laughter's so important.

**IVAN**

Life without it would be hell. And now you live in Ireland, surrounded by people who have a great sense of humour. Have they taken to you?

**NICK**

Irish people are great. Leona and I have lots of Irish friends and we have a good time. Ireland's nice. But I love going back to England, too. Leona's sister is based in Watford and her parents are just outside of Dublin in a place called Kells. Her family is fantastic. They've welcomed me into it and can laugh and joke about things that are printed about me. They're very down to earth and they're very similar to me in that respect. They're good fun and they're a loving family. Not to the degree of the American style of overdoing the sentiment with dramatic hugs and kisses, but they're very obviously affectionate and clearly care for each other. I like that. And that's something that was missing from my life when I was young and so I value it enormously. Mind you, it's a bit difficult with stepchildren, whether to kiss them and things like that. I don't because they have a different father, but I am attentive. I'll cuddle them if they need a cuddle. From my viewpoint, at the moment there's a line not to cross. That may change.

Lots of things are changing with the arrival of the baby, an event that was probably the most frightening, and at the same time the most fantastic, thing that's ever happened to me. I was so worried at times because my expectations about giving birth were totally incorrect. I expected the baby to come out and cry straight away and of course it didn't. The head came out first and there was this very eerie, quiet period while the delivery was finishing up. And I was very worried that something was wrong – and Leona was close to having a Caesarean and the whole pain thing that women go through. You just feel so inadequate. Leona, she said, 'That's the quietest I've ever seen you.' Usually I'm a terrible gobshite and I've always got an opinion on something and I'm offering it and usually getting it thrown back at me. But during that four or five hours I was struck dumb. She couldn't understand. But I had nothing to say. I just wanted to take some of that pain away from her and I couldn't.

### IVAN

Well, you've been through enough of it yourself.

### NICK

Most of my pain has been self-inflicted; I can't complain. But I think that, whatever's going on in one's life, it's always important to look for positives. Even in the Singapore jail, with the divorce, the solitary confinement, the diagnosis of cancer, I could still search out positives to give myself some focus to move towards. I think anybody should be able to do that.

## IVAN'S COMMENTARY

It is clear to me that Nick Leeson's experiences allowed him to discover some perennial truths about the nature of stress and its psychological and physiological effects. Without a shadow of doubt he has a unique perspective on life because

of what he brought upon himself. He suffered the consequences of his corrupt behaviour but also learned a lot – and
is still learning.

*Everybody* causes suffering, however, and *everybody* experiences suffering. It's the price we pay for being human. So
we can all learn from his story because, providing we live life
to the full by saying *yes* to every opportunity (as long as it
doesn't damage others), each of us develops a more aware
perspective through overcoming difficulties. And the more
stark our struggle, the sharper our view of reality becomes
and the more we see. This is what Shakespeare meant when
he said, 'Sweet are the uses of adversity'. We all need to struggle against difficulties; it is how we free up our consciousness
– de-condition it – and create something new and more real
in ourselves.

Nature sets each one of us on a course to grow up and seek
the fulfilment of our innate needs in the world, a process that
requires exactly the opposite of what is happening for many
people today, hence the rise in stress-related problems. It is
in fulfilling these innate needs, including the need to be
stretched, that we develop a sense that life is meaningful.
Whenever anything prevents these requirements being met
there will always be trouble. Nick found the inner strength to
survive and mature during his period of torment. We each of
us – no matter how challenging or stressful our situation –
can find solutions to problems by looking to our own inner
resources. I hope that more people can make the same
progress to a less selfish and more responsible mindset. We
will know we are doing this as a society when the levels of
stress-related mental illness begin to fall. This is how
progress should be measured.

# Afterword

It's been an emotional journey writing this book. I've been moved to tears a couple of times, primarily when I think of the future, but revisiting some of the darker moments in my past has not been easy. Writing – expunging my thoughts and feelings on paper – remains the best way for me to cope with difficulties. For me, talking is not always the easiest way of handling difficult feelings; it can be far too personal and, not unlike many other men, I shy away from speaking frankly about my emotions. Writing removes you at least one stage from that experience. Everything I have written about is real, and not that very different from the ordeals we all have to face at one time or another during our lifetimes. Perhaps the circumstances under which they occurred are more extreme than most of us would care to imagine, but that's the whole point – if I survived those stressful situations in those extreme conditions, then we all can.

I've learned to put things in perspective. My need to achieve, to have control and attain status has been tempered massively by my experiences, and that has been compounded a degree further through writing this book. It's a common enough pattern in business that the people who are able to delegate and retain effective control over their organisation will be the most successful and least stressed. My needs were always very much at the forefront of everything I did; unfortunately my wife and family were never that important to me before the collapse of the bank; certainly not enough for me to temper my own needs. I was hungry for success and fed voraciously wherever and whenever I could. Money was never a great motivator for me; but success and the status it brought were. More often than not this blinded me to what was going on around me and, ultimately, as the need turned to greed, it tested my basic integrity and, much to my deep embarrassment and shame, I failed the test abysmally. I could have stopped during any minute of any day and I never did. Unfortunately, I'll probably never be afforded another opportunity to put that right.

Prison was a horrific experience. Even with hindsight I'm not sure how I managed to pull myself through it. Every day was a challenge and I had to find something to get me through it, often by the skin of my teeth, only to have to start the whole process again the next day. There were even times when I'd wished the guards had been a bit more violent so that I could have used anger as a tool. Arriving at the prison gates, anger was probably the only tool that I had readily at my disposal. It's such an easy emotion to descend to, but the guards were civil, often bordering on nice, so there was no real use for anger. They followed rules, however banal, and no amount of anger was going to change the way they went about their jobs.

No society that I'm aware of has more structure or more rules to it than Singapore. It drove me mad when I had my liberty but it was just as bad when I was ensconced in my cell. Turning off the water when none had arrived drove me to total distraction but, after realising that no amount of posturing or shouting was going to change the situation, I just had to get on with it. The cell needed cleaning, and I needed washing, so we'd scrub the toilet with an old toothbrush and toothpaste, wedge a water-filled plastic bag into the toilet bowl, flush like mad and collect the water that was dispensed in order to shower and clean. It stank, but it was better than the alternative. Instances like that taught me fairly quickly that there are certain things you can have influence and control over in your life and there are others that you cannot. Every situation I find myself in is viewed in exactly the same way. If I can do something about it, I will. If I can't, I just make do and get on as best I can. Try it; it certainly cuts a lot of stress and worry out of my life.

My life now is not driven by the trappings of success. The support I received from friends and family during my time in Singapore and afterwards has cemented the importance of people – rather than status and material wealth – in my life. My emotional well-being would have been crippled if they hadn't pulled and cajoled me through that awful four-and-a-half-year period. My new wife and family offer me a future. And Mackensey's arrival has solidified that need for a future even more. I want to see him take his first steps, hear him utter his first words, arrive for his first day at school and hopefully, in the future, graduate from university. I might warn him against a career in banking, but nothing more! I'd love to see him get married and have a family of his own, but I take nothing for granted. In order to do that I have to look after my health and avoid any more of the stressful situations that may confront me in the future.

I'm certainly not stress-free – I'm not sure that state exists anywhere in the modern world – but I am certainly able to limit the number of stressors better than most. My most important focus for the future remains my health; it started nearly six years ago when I was diagnosed with colon cancer and has remained the case ever since. I am better equipped than ever to be able to do that. I believe that we all are, through accessing those human givens – the innate resources that have served us so well as a species. It's a process of discovery, though. We all live such fast-paced and stressful lives that we never have the chance to take time out to discover ways of coping. As torturous an experience as prison was, it removed me from the damaging situation I was in, and forced me to use that time to focus on myself and put things right. Caught up in the stress of everyday lives, many people find it impossible to afford themselves the luxury of self-reflection. Being constantly under too much pressure to earn money to feed their lifestyles leaves many people blinkered to the fact that it is those same lifestyles that are making them ill. My calamitous fall from grace echoed around the world and brought me huge embarrassment, but if I am grateful for one thing it is that it forced me to take that time out and reflect – and, awful as it was, no doubt prevented me keeling over with a premature heart attack caused by stress. Don't let it happen to you!

# Source Notes and Bibliography

**CHAPTER 1: The Story So Far**
'Half a million Britons experiencing work-related stress', *Health and Safety Executive*, 2004, www.hse.gov.uk/statistics /causdis/stress (The HSE is sponsored by the Department of Work and Pensions.)

**CHAPTER 2: What Is Stress?**
**Needs, Resources And Human Givens**
Gopnik, A., Kuhl, P. and Meltzoff, A. *How Babies Think: The Science of Childhood,* Weidenfeld & Nicolson, 1999
Griffin, J. and Tyrrell, I. *Human Givens: A New Approach to Emotional Health and Clear Thinking,* HG Publishing, 2003
Griffin, J. and Tyrrell, I. *Dreaming Reality: How Dreaming Keeps us Sane, or Can Drive us Mad,* HG Publishing, 2004
Kagan, J. 'Stress and coping in early development' N. Garmezy and M. Rutter (eds.) *Stress, Coping, and Development in Children,* McGraw-Hill, 1983
Konner, M. 'Universals of behavioural development in relation to brain myelination' (1991) in K. R. Gibson and A. C. Petersen (eds.), *Brain Maturation and Cognitive Development: Comparative and Cross-cultural Perspectives,* Aldine de Gruyter, 1991

Youngblade, L. M. and Belsky, J. 'Parent–child antecedents of 5-year-olds' close friendships' (1992) in *Developmental Psychology*, 28, 700–713

'In the UK, as many as one in five people are suffering from high levels of work-related stress' *Health and Safety Executive*, 2001

Ratey, J. *A User's Guide to the Brain*, Pantheon Books, 2001

Carter, R. *Mapping The Mind*, Phoenix, 2000

Cooper, L. *Handbook of Stress Medicine and Health*, Second Edition, CRC Press, 2004

Cunningham, J. B. *The Stress Management Sourcebook*, Lowell House, 2001

Martin, Paul *Counting Sheep: The Science and Pleasures of Sleep and Dreams*, HarperCollins, 2002

Holford, P. *Patrick Holford's New Optimum Nutrition Bible: The Book You Have to Read If You Care About Your Health*, Piatkus, 2004

Rossi, E. L. *The 20 Minute Break*, Jeremy Tarcher Inc., 1991

Ornstein, R. and Sobel, D. *The Healing Brain: A Radical New Approach to Staying Well*, Papermac, 1988

**CHAPTER 3: Status: Be Careful What You Strive For**

De Botton, A. *Status Anxiety*, Penguin Books, 2004

Moir, A. and Moir, B. *Why Men Don't Iron: The Real Science of Gender Studies*, HarperCollins Publishers, 1998

Gurian, M. *What Could he be Thinking? A Guide to the Mysteries of a Man's Mind*, Element, 2003

Ornstein, R. and Erlich, P. *New World New Mind: A Brilliantly Original Guide to Changing the Way We Think About the Future*, Touchstone, 1990

Csikszentmihalyi, M. *Flow: The Psychology of Happiness*, Harper & Row, 1992

Lane, R. E. *The Loss of Happiness in Market Democracies*, Yale University Press, 2000

Furedi, F. *Therapy Culture: Cultivating Vulnerability in an Uncertain Age*, Routledge, 2004

Pinker, S. *The Blank Slate: The Modern Denial of Human Nature*, Allen Lane, 2002

Hewitt, J. P. *The Myth of Self Esteem*, St Martin's Press, 1998

Emler, N. *The Costs and Causes of Low Self Worth*, The Rowntree Foundation, 2001

Bromhall, C. *The Eternal Child*, Ebury Press, 2003

Tyrrell, I. 'Exploring the CULT in culture' in *The Therapist*, editions: 1, 2, 29-32

Deikman, A. J. *Them and Us: Cult thinking and the Terrorist Threat*, Bay Tree, 2004

*Work Stress & Health: The Whitehall II Study*, commissioned by the Council of Civil Service Unions (CCSU) in collaboration with the Cabinet Office, 2004

Shah, I. *Learning How to Learn*, Octagon Press, 1978

For information on greed and the need for attention etc. see Griffin, J. and Tyrrell, I. *Human Givens: A New Approach to Emotional Health and Clear Thinking*, HG Publishing, 2003

**CHAPTER 4: Isolation and Confinement**
Winn, D. *The Manipulated Mind: Brainwashing, Conditioning and Indoctrination,* Malor Books, 2000
Tavris, C. *Anger – the Misunderstood Emotion,* Simon & Schuster, 1982
Griffin, J. and Tyrrell, I. *How to Lift Depression ... Fast (The Human Givens Approach),* HG Publishing, 2004
Griffin, J. and Tyrrell, I. *Dreaming Reality: How Dreaming Keeps us Sane, or Can Drive us Mad,* HG Publishing, 2004
Griffin, J. and Tyrrell, I. *The Therapeutic Power of Guided Imagery* (CD) MindFields College, 2005
Griffin, J. and Tyrrell, I. *Human Givens: A New Approach to Emotional Health and Clear Thinking,* HG Publishing, 2003

**CHAPTER 5: Relationships, Divorce and Loss**
Gurian, M. *What Could he be Thinking? A Guide to the Mysteries of a Man's Mind,* Element, 2003
Tannen, Deborah, *You Just Don't Understand: Women and Men in Conversation,* Virago, 2002
McGrath, E. et al. *Women and Depression,* American Psychological Association, 1990
McClure, E. 'A meta-analytic review of sex differences in facial expression processing and their development in infants, children and adolescents' *Psychological Bulletin,* 126, 2000, 424–453
Phillips, M. *The Sex-Change Society: Feminised Britain and the Neutered male,* Social Market Foundation, 1999
Goleman, D. *Emotional Intelligence: Why it can Matter More Than IQ,* Bloomsbury, 1996

Gottman, John, *Why Marriages Succeed or Fail,*
Bloomsbury, 1998
Baron-Cohen, S. *The Essential Difference: Men, Women and
the Extreme Male Brain,* Allen Lane, 2003

**CHAPTER 6: Cancer**
Martin, Paul *The Sickening Mind: Brain, Behaviour, Immunity
& Disease,* Flamingo, 1997
Blakeslee, T. R. *The Attitude Factor,* HarperCollins, 1997

**CHAPTER 7: Money Worries**
'Monty', *New Statesman,* 24 November 2003
'Half of all personal bankrupts now under 30', *Daily Mail,*
14 February, 2005
'Credit card aimed at the poor' – *Guardian* 19 February 2005
'67 million credit cards in circulation', *Metro,* 3 November 2004
UK personal lending statistics, *Datamonitor,* December 2003
Mischel, W., Shoda, Y, and Rodriguez, M. L. 'Delay of gratification
in children'(1989) in *Science,* 244, 933–937
Boyle, D. *The Tyranny of Numbers: Why Counting Can't Make
Us Happy,* Flamingo, 2001
Griffin, J. and Tyrrell, I. *Human Givens: A New Approach to
Emotional Health and Clear Thinking,* HG Publishing, 2003

**CHAPTER 8: Addiction**

Ornstein, R. *The Roots of the Self,* Harper Collins, 1995

Prochaska, J., DiClemente, C. and Norcross, J. *In Search of How People Change: Applications to Addictive Behavior, American Psychologist,* 47, 1992, 1102-1114

'Adults drinking above recommended alcohol guidelines, by ethnic group and sex,' Department of Health National Statistics, England, 1999

Aust, Rebecca; Sharp, Clare and Goulden, Chris 'Prevalence of drug use: key findings from the 2001/2002 British Crime Survey,' Home Office Research, Development and Statistics Directorate, Findings 182, 2002

'Annual Report on the UK Drug Situation,' *Drugscope,* December 2003

Thompson, Jonathan 'I guess I've become nocturnal... it's addictive but I do win money' *Independent on Sunday,* 8 August 2004

Davenport-Hines, R. *The Pursuit of Oblivion: A Global History of Narcotics 1500–2000,* Weidenfeld & Nicolson, 2001

Griffin, J. and Tyrrell, I. *Freedom from Addiction: The Secret Behind Successful Addiction Busting,* HG Publishing, 2005

Dobson, Roger 'Female sex on the rise say psychiatrists' National Council on Sexual Addiction and Compulsivity, *Independent on Sunday,* 8 August 2004

healthcreation

To get your own full assessment as in the diagram shown on page 203 of this book you will need to get a Picture of Health pack from Health Creation (see below) or do this exercise as a part of the full Health Creation Programme.

So whether it's for someone who is ill and needing a health boost, or either you or your organisation that wishes to establish a Health Creation culture at the core of all your activities, please contact me and my team on 0845-009-3366 or check out our website **www.healthcreation.co.uk**

**Prices**

The Picture of Health: self-assessment pack (120 questions) – Price: £10 (incl. VAT) (also available through Waterstones in the UK).

The Health Creation Programme: 6-month programme, 5 self-assessment exercises (incl. Picture of Health). Price: £70 (incl. VAT)

The Cancer Lifeline Kit: Message of Hope Video, Cancer Lifeline Programme workbook, 3 audio CDs, two guidebooks on cancer medicine and alternative treatments, Carer's Guide, Health Creation Programme and Cancer Lifeline Recipe Cards. Price: £150 (incl. VAT)

Health Creation in Business: Full consultancy process for individuals, teams and entire organisations wishing to make positive health changes – prices on application

# THE HUMAN GIVENS FOUNDATION

THE
## HUMAN GIVENS
## FOUNDATION

The human givens approach draws on scientific findings, gathered mainly over the last few decades, about how human beings function, and refers to our basic emotional needs (such as for attention, security, connection and control), and the innate resources we have for meeting them (such as memory, imagination, problem solving abilities and complementary thinking styles). It is when these emotional needs are not met, or our resources are used incorrectly, that individuals suffer mental distress or fail to fulfil their potential.

The HGF supports psychological/social regeneration programmes that foster practical initiatives by those endeavouring to use up-to-date knowledge about the givens of human nature in practical ways, particularly in fields where developing life skills is vital, such as in education, psychotherapy, counselling, health, social work, industrial relations and diplomacy.

The work of the Foundation is directed at the following areas:

- to set up and administer centres where persons suffering from mental illness of any description can be helped more effectively

- to develop model schools that work in line with what is now known about how children and adults really learn

- to conduct further research into how all organisations can work in tune with the givens of human nature

- to advance public education of mental health care

These initiatives require considerable funding which HGF is actively seeking.

HGF is a charity and welcomes members and offers of financial and in-kind support. MindFields College, which trains over 12,500 professionals a year, provides seminars and workshops and in-house training days focusing on the human givens approach, and offers a diploma course for those wanting more in depth education on the topics.
(Tel: 01323 811440 for a prospectus.)

For more information go to: **www.hgfoundation.com** and **www.mindfields.org.uk**

# How to discover more about the new school of psychology discussed in this book

www.humangivens.com

Griffin, Joe and Tyrrell, Ivan, *Human Givens: A New Approach to Emotional Health and Clear Thinking*, HG Publishing, 2004

Griffin, Joe and Tyrrell, Ivan, *How to Lift Depression – Fast: The Human Givens Approach*, HG Publishing, 2004

Griffin, Joe and Tyrrell, Ivan, *Freedom from Addiction: The Secret Behind Successful Addiction Busting*, HG Publishing, 2005

# What people have said about the Human Givens:

'A quiet revolution.' *New Scientist*

'It's absolutely the right way forward.' BBC Radio 4, *All in the Mind*

'An entirely attainable and reasonable road map for good mental health.' *Irish Examiner*

'Insights of sufficient power to completely revolutionise our approach to parenting, teaching and the caring professions.' Dr Nick Baylis, Cambridge University

'A wonderfully fresh and stimulating view ... it will deepen and widen every reader's perspective.' Arthur J. Deikman, Clinical Professor of Psychiatry, University of California

'Innovative perspectives on promoting effective living ... new templates for understanding how to unlock the best in human nature.' Dr Jeffrey K Zeig

'Advances psychology as much as the introduction of the Arabic numeric system with its zero digit advanced mathematics.' *Washington Times*

'Important original work ... both aesthetically pleasing and of immense practical use ... has great relevance to all areas of life ... could save (tax payers) millions of pounds.' Dr Farouk Okhai, Consultant Psychiatrist in Psychotherapy

'A refreshing alternative to reams of expensive psychobabble.' *Big Issue*

# Index

**Disclaimer**
Virgin Books Ltd has no affiliation with the companies advertising products and services in this book and accepts no responsibility for dissatisfaction arising out of contact with them.